wsey

Cambridge International AS & A Level

Global Perspectives & Research

Coursebook

CAMBRIDGE
UNIVERSITY PRESS

CAMBRIDGE
UNIVERSITY PRESS

University Printing House, Cambridge CB2 8BS, United Kingdom

One Liberty Plaza, 20th Floor, New York, NY 10006, USA

477 Williamstown Road, Port Melbourne, VIC 3207, Australia

314–321, 3rd Floor, Plot 3, Splendor Forum, Jasola District Centre, New Delhi – 110025, India

79 Anson Road, #06–04/06, Singapore 079906

Cambridge University Press is part of the University of Cambridge.

It furthers the University's mission by disseminating knowledge in the pursuit of education, learning and research at the highest international levels of excellence.

Information on this title: www.cambridge.org

First published 2017

20 19 18 17 16 15 14 13 12 11 10 9 8 7 6 5 4

Printed in Malaysia by Vivar Printing

A catalogue record for this publication is available from the British Library

ISBN 978-1-107-56081-9 Paperback

ISBN 978-1-108-43169-9 Cambridge Elevate edition (2 years)

ISBN 978-1-107-56085-7 Digital edition

....

....

All exam-style questions and answers were written by the author.

Contents

Introduction

Who is this book for?

This book is designed to support students and teachers with the Cambridge International AS & A Level Global Perspectives & Research syllabus (9239). Global Perspectives & Research is an unusual course in that it has several distinctive purposes:

- It is designed to be global in scope, introducing you to issues which affect a range of different people across the world, and are of sharp contemporary relevance for our planet in the 21st century.

- It encourages you to explore different perspectives – alternative ways of seeing particular situations – and to appreciate that there is usually more than one perspective on any issue we encounter.

- Although intended to be a valuable experience in itself, it is also intended to support the development of academic skills which you can apply to other subjects you are doing, and that will also support you with the next stage of education or work.

By completing this course, you will acquire specific ways of working and attitudes to study that will change the way you approach all of your academic studies, not just this AS or A Level.

The nature of Cambridge Global Perspectives®

Global Perspectives & Research is unlike most AS & A Level courses in that it is cumulative and integrated. It is cumulative in that each stage builds on the previous one, and your success in each of the assessments depends in a very direct way on the ones you have previously completed, and the work you have done before. It is integrated in that the course as a whole fits very closely together, and the skills and attitudes you learn will depend on everything that you have done, and not individual units or assessments taken separately.

The ideas that each stage of the course builds on the one before, and that the whole of the course can be seen together, are brought together in a metaphor called the Critical Path. This is introduced in detail in Chapter 1, but the book will continue to use it as a representation of the skills you are developing and how they fit together. It is a metaphor because it uses the idea of a path as a representation of a route towards a destination, but one which connects that end point with where we started from, and shows how each step along the route builds on the one that went before. It is a 'critical' path because the linked skills you will be building up will encourage you to be critical, or to question what you find around you.

How to use this book

Because of the nature of the course, this is not the sort of book that you can just dip into in order to find out how to accomplish a specific task, or to retrieve a particular piece of information you need. The first chapter is an essential starting point, because it explains the idea of the Critical Path and models how it works in bringing together a set of linked skills and activities to interrogate and explore questions of global relevance. Chapter 1 then needs to be read together with Chapters 2 and 3: these contain teaching on core skills from the Critical Path which are most immediately useful for tackling the texts and questions you will find in the written examination paper. However, they are equally essential for all of the other components, and the later chapters will make less sense if you are not familiar with what is contained within the first three.

Chapters 4 and 5 are focused on researching for and writing the essay. Chapters 6, 7 and 8 each focus on an aspect of the team project. Once you are familiar with the approach of the Critical Path and its core skills, it will then be possible to read either of these sets of chapters as a unit in order to prepare for the other components. By working through to the end of Chapter 8 you will have covered everything required for the AS if your learning aim is to complete that only.

In order to also undertake the A Level, you will also need to complete the research report, which is covered in Chapter 9. It is important to realise, however, that the Global Perspectives & Research A Level is also staged: this means that the requirements of the research report assume that you have previously experienced all three of the AS components. The report requires you to bring together all of the skills and approaches from the AS components and apply them in one piece of work. As the final stretch of the Critical Path, you can embark on the report with confidence once you have worked through everything else the course has to offer.

Key features of this book

Each chapter contains the following features, designed to help you get the most from your study.

Learning aims

By the end of this chapter, you should be able to:

- understand the relationship between skills and knowledge
- ask questions about a number of different global issues
- explain the Critical Path
- make use of the Critical Path to understand issues
- relate the Critical Path to the core academic skills of analysis and evaluation
- reflect on how the Critical Path can be used to develop skills and make decisions about issues and debates.

Learning aims: Each chapter begins with a short list of the areas of learning aims for you to achieve. For example, these are the learning aims for Chapter 1.

Activities: Activities are designed so that you can work independently, in pairs or in small groups. There may also be occasions when a teacher wants to use one or more of the activities with students at the same time, or as a task for you to complete alone or together outside the classroom.

ACTIVITY 1.01

1 Make a list of some of the **knowledge** you have acquired from your studies so far. This might include scientific knowledge, such as the boiling point of water, knowledge about different countries and cultures, or knowledge of specific information which is useful in the study of a subject.

2 Now make a list of some **skills** you think you already have as a student. These might be skills of writing, note-taking or organising your study notes and revision, or skills you have in speaking or interacting with others.

Differentiated practice: Chapters 2–8 also have fully differentiated practice sections at the end of each chapter on green pages. These sections are differentiated at three levels: developing, establishing and enhancing. These allow you to practise the skills you have acquired and developed throughout the chapter.

Practising presentations for your team project

This section of the chapter is divided into three: firstly, establishing the effectiveness of your presentation, secondly, developing the effectiveness of your presentation and finally, enhancing the effectiveness of your presentation. Each section is designed to build on the one before. You can either work through each section in turn or choose the section that you feel is at the most appropriate level for you.

You should also see a progression of difficulty through the three levels, but they are also aligned in this chapter to the distinctive skills we have established.

These sections use a variety of topics from the Cambridge International AS & A Level Global Perspectives & Research syllabus.

Establishing effective presentations

Based on what you have read in this chapter, take an inventory of your presentational skills.

- What can you do well already, and what evidence do you have for this from your previous experience with giving presentations?
- What do you still need to work on with your presentational skills and how will you do that?

Developing effective presentations

Plan out the structure of your presentation and make notes on what you will say. Do not try to produce a script, but instead use a mind-map or bullet points to produce a detailed summary which you can then transfer onto cue cards to support your presentation.

Enhancing effective presentations

Choose a type of visual aid or aspect of personal performance from this chapter which you have not tried before. Alternatively, select a method you have used and take advantage of the ideas about where to use it in a new way. How can you develop this to creatively present the explanations and arguments in your presentation?

Discussion point

Talk to a group of other students (who may or may not be following the Global Perspectives & Research course) about your experiences of working together with people.

Considering your past experiences and sharing your feelings is an important first step towards the work you will do to develop your collaborative skills on this course.

Discussion points: The purpose of discussion points is to enable you to discuss your own thoughts and ideas with someone else, so that you not only get different opinions but can also clarify your own thinking by saying things out loud.

Reflection points: Reflection points are included throughout the book so that you have the chance to think about how your skills are developing and how they can be applied.

Reflection: Have there been occasions in your life, in any context, where you have had to combine information from a number of different places in order to get something done or find something out?

KEY TERM

analysis: the breakdown of something into smaller parts in order to understand it more clearly

Key terms: Key terms are included throughout the text and provide clear and straightforward explanations of the most important terms in each chapter.

Critical Path links: Each chapter also contains a diagram that indicates which part of the Critical Path is highlighted within the chapter. This example shows that Deconstruction will be covered in the chapter.

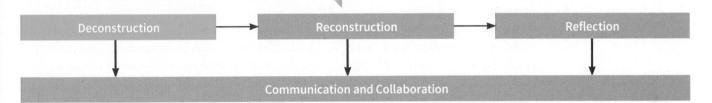

Summary: There is a summary at the end of each chapter to help you review what you have learnt.

Summary

In this chapter, we have:

- identified why skills are important, and considered the focus of the Global Perspectives & Research course on developing skills
- considered what issues are in a global context, and practised using those skills to explore, discuss and make decisions on a number of example issues together in groups, as well as reflecting upon and communicating those decisions
- formally identified this process as something called the Critical Path, and showed how this path relates to each stage and type of learning you will undertake for Global Perspectives & Research
- used the Critical Path to provide a roadmap for the whole of this book and to show how each chapter will help you to

develop particular skills and prepare for specific examined assessments.

The skills contained in the Critical Path and discussed in this chapter will form the basis of your learning throughout your Global Perspectives & Research course. When you did Activity 1.03 you covered all the areas of this process. Becoming a more effective student of Global Perspectives & Research will now involve repeating and developing those skills in more detail and in a range of different contexts. It will be through a process of repetition – practising, getting feedback, identifying strengths and weaknesses, then testing yourself again in new contexts – that you will become a fully competent student of Global Perspectives & Research. It is the aim of this book to help you achieve that goal.

Acknowledgements

The authors and publishers acknowledge the following sources of copyright material and are grateful for the permissions granted. While every effort has been made, it has not always been possible to identify the sources of all the material used, or to trace all copyright holders. If any omissions are brought to our notice, we will be happy to include the appropriate acknowledgements on reprinting.

Chapter 2 Activity 2.02 entry for 'Internet' from Encyclopaedia Britannica; Activity 2.06 from 'Graffiti is young, cool, creative – let it happen, by Lady Pink in the New York Times, July 2014; Activity 2.07 from 'Graffiti is a public good, even as it challenges the law' by Lu Olivero in the New York Times, July 2014; article extract 'Why the UK should embrace fracking' by Chris Faulkner in the Guardian, copyright Guardian News & Media Ltd 2017; from 'Fracking', Greenpeace www.greenpeace.org; Activity 2.12 source 1 from 'Floody Obvious' (The Sun Says, 2016), The Sun, © News Syndication; Activity 2.12 source 2 from 'The Guardian view on the heatwave: still hope on climate change', The Guardian, Copyright Guardian News & Media Ltd 2017; Activity 2.12 source 3 from 'Changing the climate debate' by Bjorn Lomborg, Prospect Magazine, November 2007; Deconstruction document 1 from 'Here are the three biggest threats to the world right now' by Mehreen Khan, January 2016 © The Telegraph 2016; Deconstruction deocumner 2 from 'Migration is now a fact of life…deal with it – The City View' from City A.M. October 2015; Chapter 3 Activity 3.02 extract 1 from 'Achieving Gender Equality: When Everyone Wins' by Charlotta Sparre for Daily News Egypt, October 2015; Activity 3.02 extract 2 from 'Gender equality' from UNESCAP; Activity 3.03 extract 1 from 'Let's just be honest and allow drugs in sport' by James Kirkup, June 2015 © The Telegraph 2016; Activity 3.03 extract 2 from 'Why it's time to legalise doping in athletics' by Julian Savulescu (August 2015) with permission from The Conversation; extract from 'How Costa Rica runs on renewable energy - and why it's so hard to replicate' by Aimee Meade, September 2017, The Independent; Deconstruction document 1 & 2 letters by Claire Robinson and Mark Lynas in the Independent, March 2015; Deconstruction document 1 from 'Fear about GM crops is not backed up by facts', by William Reville, July 2015 in The Irish Times, with permission from the author William Reville; Deconstruction document 2 from 'Approach GM foods with caution, not total rejection' by Fr Dr John M M Kamweri, June 2015 in The Observer (Kampala)

Thanks to the following for permission to reproduce images:

Cover Bee Smith/Getty Images; Inside (in order of appearance) oversnap/Getty Images; Hans-Peter Merten/Getty Images; Anatoliy Babiy/Getty Images; Peter Cade/Getty Images; Han Lans/Getty Images; Roy Scott/Getty Images; Thomas Imo/Photothek via Getty Images; DanielAzocar/Getty Images; Andreas Guskos/Getty Images; John Wildgoose/Getty Images; Tom Merton/Getty Images; arabianEye arabianEye/Getty Images; Roy Mehta/Getty Images; Robert Daly/Getty Images; David Crunelle/EyeEm/Getty Images; vgajic/Getty Images; Jack Taylor/Getty Images; Colin Anderson/Getty Images; OJO Images/Tom Merton/Getty Images; asiseeit/Getty Images; Echo/Getty Images; endopack/Getty Images; Cultura RM Exclusive/Frank and Helena/Getty Images; Robert Daly/Getty Images; filadendron/Getty Images; FatCamera/Getty Images; Rob Atkins/Getty Images; HaizhanZheng/Getty Images; Dmitry Goygel-sokol/Getty Images; FatCamera/Getty Images; Nisian Hughes/Getty Images; David Schaffer/Getty Images; Adrianko/Getty Images; Paul Taylor/Getty Images; Kentaroo Tryman/Getty Images; Peter Muller/Getty Images; Dave and Les Jacobs/Getty Images; PeopleImages/Getty Images

Chapter 1
Getting started with the Critical Path

Learning aims

By the end of this chapter, you should be able to:

- understand the relationship between skills and knowledge
- ask questions about a number of different global issues
- explain the Critical Path
- make use of the Critical Path to understand issues
- relate the Critical Path to the core academic skills of analysis and evaluation
- reflect on how the Critical Path can be used to develop skills and make decisions about issues and debates.

This chapter will support you with all of the assessed components of Global Perspectives & Research: written exam answers, essays, team projects and your research report.

The Critical Path consists of three linked steps which build on one another as types of thinking, and two closely associated skills of expression which support them:

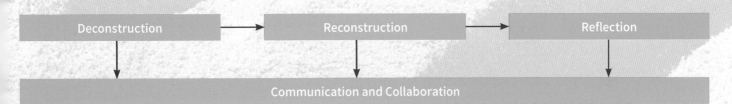

Introduction

We live in a complex and ever-changing world. The amount of information in existence, and our access to it on a daily basis, would have baffled previous generations. This information is **global** both in its scale across the planet, and in its **local** variety in many different places.

When we refer to something as 'global', we are not only concerned with things that relate to the whole globe, or world, at once. Global insights also come from comparing the situation in different global locations so that we understand the world through its diversity. Understanding global diversity, however, also means having a sharp sense of the local. When we study the local, we are looking at a specific place, not the world as a whole. This might be our own locality (our town, region or country), or concerns which are local to other places or cultures but not our own.

All of this variety also means that we will encounter a number of different, and frequently conflicting, points of view. Deciding who might be correct, and what we think ourselves, is not an easy task. We need some techniques which will enable us to discover what people think, why they believe what they do, and how we might develop, justify and present our own points of view.

KEY TERMS

global: pertaining to the world as a whole, either looked at overall, or compared in its diversity

local: relating to specific places in the world looked at individually. These might be villages, towns, regions or countries.

skills: any mental or physical abilities you can improve through practising them

knowledge: our understanding of facts or other information

1.01 Skills and knowledge

A Level Global Perspectives & Research differs from most other subjects which you might study. This is because it helps students to develop **skills** rather than testing the recall of specific **knowledge**. It is designed to help you with some tools and approaches to engage with the complexity of the modern world, to understand the views of others and to help you put forward your own.

Being skilled means having the ability to do something effectively. It is any mental or physical ability in which you can become expert through practice or learning.

Knowledge is often seen as another word for the information or facts we possess about the world, as distinct from being skilled. However, knowledge and skills could be said to be closely related in a number of ways. Knowledge in the sense in which we are interested is (according to the *Shorter Oxford English Dictionary*) 'understanding of or information about a subject that you get by experience or study'. Being skilled could be said to be having developed the ability to understand a subject through practice. In this sense, skills are the tools we need to use knowledge effectively. We can improve our skills by using them repeatedly and reflecting on how we have used them in order to handle knowledge purposefully.

ACTIVITY 1.01

1   Make a list of some of the **knowledge** you have acquired from your studies so far. This might include scientific knowledge, such as the boiling point of water, knowledge about different countries and cultures, or knowledge of specific information which is useful in the study of a subject.

2   Now make a list of some **skills** you think you already have as a student. These might be skills of writing, note-taking or organising your study notes and revision, or skills you have in speaking or interacting with others.

Reflection: What do you think the main differences are between skills and knowledge? Which is more important, and do we need both?

1.02 Global issues

Global Perspectives & Research starts with noticing **issues** in the world around us. Let's begin by exploring one of these.

What can we use to power our lives? For most of the world, the answer is fossil fuels such as oil, gas or coal. For motor transport, heat and light, and electronic devices of all kinds, there is no clear alternative that would keep everyone and everything running. Yet these sources of energy have some clear limitations. Firstly, they are finite: laid down in the earth over millions of years, at our current rates of usage we will have used all of them up in a century or two at best, and possibly much more quickly than that. Secondly, many argue that they are changing our climate: their emission of carbon dioxide into the atmosphere is warming the planet at rates which far exceed previous periods of natural climate change and risk catastrophic consequences of flooding and drought in different parts of the world. Yet many of the proposed solutions of renewable energy have their own problems: would wind, wave or solar power produce enough to fill the gap, and does the other alternative – nuclear power – carry too many risks of its own? Perhaps the best solution is for communities to change their ways of life so they use less energy in the first place.

KEY TERM

issue: a topic or idea of importance locally or globally

ACTIVITY 1.02

1 The issue here is where we should get our energy from. What is your view? Write down your ideas or discuss them with someone else.

2 From the alternatives listed, which do you think is the best source of energy? Perhaps you have another alternative you would like to suggest, or think we should continue to use fossil fuels for as long as we can.

   Another response might be to ask whether we should be using as much energy in the first place, or even to question who 'we' is here. Industrialised countries, located mostly in the northern hemisphere, use by far the most energy, although some rapidly industrialising countries, such as Brazil and China, are catching up fast. On the other hand, many countries in the developing world use far less.

   Consider these options and use them to develop your responses to (1) in more detail.

Reflection: We now have a range of possible responses to this issue. Are they all mutually contradictory, or could some be reconciled so that they support one another? For example, is it possible that the world could switch to several different forms of alternative energy, depending on local circumstances? On the other hand, the views of those who see fossil fuels as the only realistic source of energy for the industrialised world at least may always be in conflict with those who argue that they are too polluting.

How can we decide between these alternatives, or can we do so at all? Are there additional details we could find out to resolve the disagreements, or at least better justify each view, and where would that information come from?

ACTIVITY 1.03

Read through the following four issues. If you are working in groups, you might want to take one each and present your findings to the whole class. For each issue, consider the following points:

- What is your own opinion about this issue?
- Are there other possible opinions, or if you are working in a group, can you make a list of the opinions of each member of the group?
- Where different opinions demonstrate disagreements, can you resolve these by reaching a compromise?
- What more could you find out about this issue in order to reach a more considered opinion?

Issue 1: Online communities

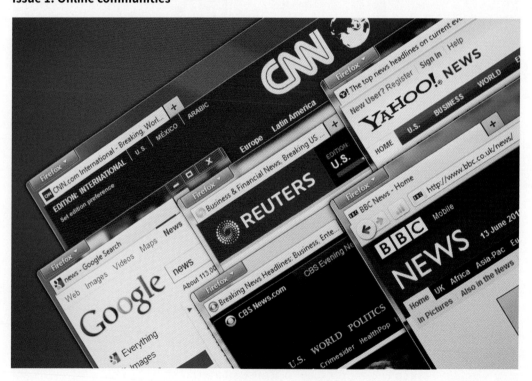

The growth of the internet has transformed social, cultural and economic life in ways that would have been inconceivable even a few decades ago. Online communities such as Facebook, LinkedIn and Twitter have allowed people to present themselves, find and remain connected to others in ways which would have previously been difficult or impossible. Information and learning are now available on a near-ubiquitous level, simply by typing a term into a search engine, signing up for a discussion list or enrolling in an online educational course. The ability to publish and consume knowledge has also become highly democratic, crossing social groups and international boundaries in a way that is almost entirely outside the control of the authorities.

This power to construct and share your identity, however, has also brought about the ability to conceal it. Is the fellow 16-year-old girl you are messaging actually a 25-year-old woman – or a 50-year-old man? The definition of 'community' has also shifted in less appealing ways. The student community, or game-playing community, or YouTube-watching community can helpfully extend our notion of the term in ways not limited by geography. However, other 'communities' have used the anonymity of the internet to share and spread offensive or illegal material. The internet has also become the favoured medium for radical political groups, often advocating intolerance or violence, to disseminate their ideas.

Discussion point
- Does it matter if people present themselves online differently to how they are in person?
- How comfortable are you with these definitions of 'community'?

Issue 2: Quality of life

Deconstruction

Reconstruction

Reflection

Communication and Collaboration

Deconstruction

Reconstruction

Reflection

Communication and Collaboration

What makes people happiest? One answer might be money, but evidence from countries in the developed world suggests that this might not always be the case. In recent years, many countries in Europe and America have suffered from an increased threat of terrorism, which has produced a sense of personal insecurity. Despite similar levels of wealth, different countries can also vary in the availability of social and healthcare services, meaning that the position of individual citizens can be much more precarious, especially if they experience unemployment, or have not insured themselves against risks.

Work–life balance can also play a role: the advanced industrialised economies might be able to generate much more money, but in order to do so many individuals are encouraged to make themselves available 24 hours a day, 7 days a week, receiving messages on their smartphones. Even climate can also be a factor, as the dark winter nights in some parts of the world can cause psychological disorders related to the level of available light, especially if people have to get up early or come back late in order to travel to work.

Discussion point

- What is your view of the most significant factors influencing personal happiness?
- Does money matter most in the end, or does the individual's level of personal security, or freedom, play a greater role?
- To be happy, is it necessary to be able to balance work with family, or does it all come down to geographical location?
- What does happiness mean?

Issue 3: Global trade

World trade currents

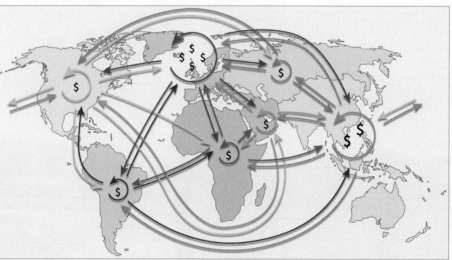

Many of the manufactured goods purchased in Europe or North America are made in China or the Indian subcontinent. Sometimes this means that an item of clothing might cost more to repair, or even to dry clean, than it was to buy in the first place. For many electronic items, such as laptop computers or smartphones, the price of the individual product may be many times more than the monthly wage of the worker who assembled it.

Yet, especially for electronic devices purchased on contract, it can often make more financial sense for the consumer to throw it away after a couple of years in favour of a slightly

Deconstruction

Reconstruction

Reflection

Communication and Collaboration

upgraded model. Those discarded phones often end up back in the developing world, in vast waste dumps, where the metals and chemicals used in their manufacture slowly pollute the environment and make people sick.

Discussion point

- Do you consider these sorts of relationships to be an inevitable part of global trade?
- Should factors such as the environment, human health, or the gap between rich and poor play a greater role in international relations, whatever the cost?

Issue 4: Healthcare

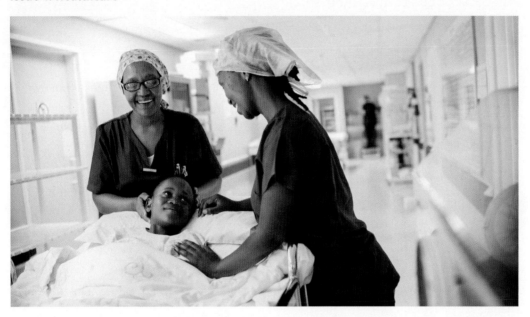

In some countries, such as the United Kingdom, most aspects of healthcare are publicly funded, and made free at the point of use through a government-backed health service. This is an enormous benefit to many people: medical treatment is related to need, rather than the ability to pay. However, getting treatment under such systems can mean a wait of many months, particularly for hospital appointments and surgical procedures. Some more recent (and expensive) drugs are also not available, even though they have been shown to help some people. Others have expressed their concern about the conditions (especially in terms of hygiene) of hospital wards, and the general standards of care available.

Some other countries, for example the United States of America, have a healthcare system based on private health insurance. There are no limits on the range of treatments available, no compromises on the standard of care and no significant waiting lists – provided you have the ability to pay. If your financial resources are more limited, you will receive considerably less, or perhaps no medical treatment at all, however ill you are. Yet when former President Obama introduced a system in the US with more publicly controlled elements and the requirement for everyone to have the option of reasonably priced health insurance, he met fierce political opposition.

Discussion point

- What is the fairest system of healthcare, and is this the same as the most effective one?
- Does government healthcare place unacceptable limits on our ability to choose our own medical treatments?
- What about countries where little or no modern healthcare is available – public or private?

Deconstruction

Reconstruction

Reflection

Communication and Collaboration

Reflection: What do you think you learnt from Activity 1.03? What process did you follow to reach conclusions, and were there any barriers you needed to overcome?

1.03 Following the Critical Path

The Critical Path process

If you did Activity 1.03 yourself, or discussed it in groups with other students, you may find that you had to do something like this:

1 *Identify* the issue and your own opinion about it.
2 *Explore* alternative viewpoints, especially those which came from other members of your group.
3 *Consider* the strengths and weaknesses of each point of view in order to make your own judgements.
4 *Communicate* the results of this process to others, either by making personal notes or explaining it to other people in your group or class.

Each of these activities needs to be undertaken in order, and each one builds on the next. Before being able to say anything about the issue, we need to *identify* it first. This allows us to decide what we are responding to, what we want to say and what that might mean.

When we know what we have identified, then we can *explore* alternative points of view, measuring how they differ from our own responses. These might include information and ideas we find from elsewhere.

All this then allows us to *consider* the extent to which those other viewpoints might make us change or develop our own.

We can *communicate* the results of this process at the end to others, by speaking or by writing, in a report, essay or piece of reflective writing.

Our audience is important, as any communication involves a relationship, or *collaboration*, with other people – whether we have ever met them or not. In truth, both the communication and the collaboration do not occur only at the end of the process. Just as, when discussing the issues in the activity, you may have been working with others from the start, you will also have been undertaking many separate and individual acts of communication along the way.

Discussion point

- Of these four steps, which did you find easiest, and which did you find most challenging to complete?
- What do you think the effect is of combining the steps so that they build on each other?

Discuss your answers to these questions with your teacher and other members of your class.

In embarking on this path and following this course of linked tasks to complete Activity 1.03, you have in fact demonstrated all the skills required of you by A Level Global Perspectives & Research. As with any skill, repeated practice will improve the precision and detail of your performance of it. You will also need to be able to explore how you can follow the path in a variety of different contexts: answering formal questions in an examination, researching and writing essays, working with groups of other people, giving oral presentations to an audience and putting together an extended research report. However, the path itself, and its skills, will remain the same.

In Global Perspectives & Research, we call this path the **Critical Path**. The course develops and tests your ability to perform the skills associated with each stage of the path and to combine them together in order to carry out typical academic or professional tasks. In this sense, mastering the Critical Path will give you a core set of competencies for the other International A Levels, or equivalent courses, you are also following.

Deconstruction

Deconstruction is what you do first, and involves answering some questions about what you are looking at:

- What is the issue you are investigating?
- Are there different points of view about this issue?
- Who is saying what? Where are they saying it? This might be in newspapers, magazines, books or other kinds of source.
- Where is the evidence that will enable you to reach your own answers?

You may notice that all of these questions have something in common: they require **analysis**. Analysis literally means 'breaking down' (from the Greek term *analusis*: 'breaking apart' or 'loosening'). It is one of the most important skills A Level students need to have. We are breaking down what we are doing into issues, views, sources and evidence. By doing this we can see its inner workings more clearly and precisely.

Even when you have answered these questions, you will not be finished. As well as breaking down views, sources and evidence, we need to make some judgements about how useful or convincing they are:

- How persuasive is that point of view?
- How convincing is the person, organisation or publication which presents it?
- How effectively is it supported by evidence?

In doing so, you will not only be analysing issues, views and evidence, you will be engaging in **evaluation**. When we evaluate something, we are making judgements on its value. This involves measuring its strengths and weaknesses in order to make a decision on how convincing or useful it is for the task in hand. These questions of evaluation will be broken down further and discussed in more detail in Chapter 2.

Reflection: Are there examples from your previous experience where you have had to analyse or evaluate? How did you find this?

Reconstruction

Reconstruction follows from deconstruction as the next stage on the path. They are closely related to one another, but while deconstruction works inwards, measuring and weighing up individual views, sources and evidence, reconstruction faces outwards. Interestingly, another term for reconstruction is **synthesis**. This is the opposite of analysis and comes from the Greek verb *syntithenai*, 'to put together' or 'to combine'. When we reconstruct, we are putting back together on a larger scale what has been broken apart by deconstruction. Rather than just looking at one point of view, reconstruction is concerned with **debates**: how might that view be challenged, and what are the alternatives? Finally, reconstruction is also interested in putting together views, sources and evidence into larger groupings which share something in common.

KEY TERM

analysis: the breakdown of something into smaller parts in order to understand it more clearly

KEY TERMS

evaluation: an identification of the strengths and weaknesses of something in order to make a judgement about it

synthesis: the combining of more than one thing together in order to understand them more effectively by exploring their differences and similarities

debate: the confrontation of opposing views on an issue, where each tries to show they are more convincing than the others

Deconstruction

Reconstruction

Reflection

Communication and Collaboration

Some of the questions we might ask here include:

- Who would agree or disagree with this view and why?
- Where else would we find additional evidence in support of this view?
- Why does more than one person or organisation subscribe to this view?
- What leads individuals or organisations to support one view more than another?
- Which approaches to issues seem stronger or more convincing, and why?

KEY TERM

perspective: a coherent worldview in response to an issue

Chapter 3 will combine reconstruction with deconstruction to show how these questions can be answered. It will also introduce the idea of **perspectives**: as the title of this course suggests, these are central to the skills we are trying to develop. The organisation of points of view into shared and opposing groups is key. (Perspectives are discussed in more detail in Chapter 3.)

Reflection: Have there been occasions in your life, in any context, where you have had to combine information from a number of different places in order to get something done or find something out?

Reflection

Reflection has several different, but equally important, meanings on the Critical Path:

1 Reflection is firstly about considering what you think, and why. Which view is strongest? Which approach is better? Which evidence is more convincing? Being able to look carefully at what you have found out, consider it, and make a judgement is one of the most important outcomes of this course, and doing it well depends on its close relationship with the stages of deconstruction and reconstruction. Reflection is not the same as just having an opinion, and it needs to be supported by the views and evidence you have already broken down and grouped together.

2 Reflection also has a second sense as part of your studies on this course. You are encouraged, all the time, to reflect on what you are doing and how you are working. This includes your own learning, but also your experiences of working together with others, especially in team projects. This type of reflection identifies and weighs up what you have achieved so you can measure the learning you have already achieved and perform better in similar situations in the future.

Chapter 4 explores the first type of reflection, focusing on the kind of thinking and judgements you will need to make when writing essays, and how this relies on what you have already deconstructed and reconstructed. Chapter 8 is concerned with the second type of reflection, both in your general development as a learner and for the assessed reflective paper you are asked to write on the work you have done for the team project.

Communication and collaboration

We will now finally deal with *communication* and *collaboration*, not because they come at the end of the process, but because they inform every stage, whether they are assessed there as part of the A Level or not.

Communication has a number of different forms, depending on how and where you are doing it:

- Firstly, by following this course, you will become more effective at communicating in writing using formal, academic formats. One key format you will need to produce successfully is the essay, and in doing so you will need to be able to communicate appropriately and effectively in this form.

- Secondly, you will also develop your skills of individual, oral communication by giving a formal presentation as part of the team project. This will be your opportunity to effectively communicate your ideas to an audience for up to eight minutes, using appropriate techniques and resources to make your message as compelling as possible. This is an important skill for life, both in many university courses and in employment, where you will often be expected to formally present to your peers, those you manage or people who are more senior than you.

Chapter 5 specifically focuses on the skills of written communication you need for writing a formal, academic essay. Chapter 7 gives lots of detailed advice and activities to help you learn and practise the skills you will need to deliver an effective oral presentation.

Collaboration is a specialised form of interpersonal communication and working. It is a general term for the skills and attitudes required by people when they work together to achieve a shared aim, or use the work of others in their team to improve their own individual learning and performance.

Human beings are social animals, and we would achieve very little if we worked entirely on our own, without the help or contribution of others. This is especially the case in an educational setting: think about the different ways, every day, in which you collaborate with the teacher and other students in every class you are part of, whether Global Perspectives & Research or other subjects. This will continue in university or the workplace, and this course is designed to help with developing those skills.

You are also, however, asked to collaborate in a more specific way when you undertake the team project. Although your final presentation will be an individual performance reflecting your own views and approach, it will rely in part on the common issue and collaborative research you have undertaken as a team with other students. Effective collaboration here is something which will make this task less challenging. When you write your reflective paper as part of the team project, you will not only be required to reflect on your individual learning, you will also be asked to consider how effectively you worked with your other team members. Knowing something about effective collaboration in a professional setting and how to measure this will therefore be very useful when you come to write that reflective paper.

Chapter 6 is devoted to the question of collaboration. This is mainly focused on the collaboration that will be expected of you while undertaking the team project, and how to make effective judgements on the quality of that collaboration. However, it also has lessons you can apply to any collaborative activity, both in your learning for other parts of the course, and in your education and life more broadly.

Discussion point

Talk to a group of other students (who may or may not be following the Global Perspectives & Research course) about your experiences of working together with people.

Considering your past experiences and sharing your feelings is an important first step towards the work you will do to develop your collaborative skills on this course.

Deconstruction

Reconstruction

Reflection

Communication and Collaboration

A note on the research report and the Critical Path

The work you will do on the written paper, essay and team project do not only lead to an AS in Global Perspectives & Research. They are an essential preparation for your research report. This will be dealt with in detail in Chapter 9, the final chapter of this book. At this stage, however, it is worth noting that this also means that the various stages of the Critical Path come together to reach the path's destination: the extended report on the thinking and research you will have done for the topic you have selected. As such, it will be your opportunity to demonstrate how well you can combine deconstruction, reconstruction, reflection, communication and even collaboration in undertaking an academic project you have chosen for yourself.

Summary

In this chapter, we have:

- identified why skills are important, and considered the focus of the Global Perspectives & Research course on developing skills

- considered what issues are in a global context, and practised using those skills to explore, discuss and make decisions on a number of example issues together in groups, as well as reflecting upon and communicating those decisions

- formally identified this process as something called the Critical Path, and showed how this path relates to each stage and type of learning you will undertake for Global Perspectives & Research

- used the Critical Path to provide a roadmap for the whole of this book and to show how each chapter will help you to

develop particular skills and prepare for specific examined assessments.

The skills contained in the Critical Path and discussed in this chapter will form the basis of your learning throughout your Global Perspectives & Research course. When you did Activity 1.03 you covered all the areas of this process. Becoming a more effective student of Global Perspectives & Research will now involve repeating and developing those skills in more detail and in a range of different contexts. It will be through a process of repetition – practising, getting feedback, identifying strengths and weaknesses, then testing yourself again in new contexts – that you will become a fully competent student of Global Perspectives & Research. It is the aim of this book to help you achieve that goal.

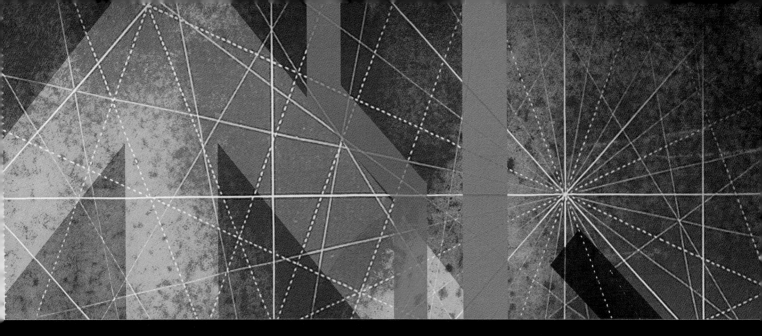

Chapter 2
Introducing deconstruction: analysing and evaluating arguments and evidence

Learning aims

By the end of this chapter, you should be able to:

- understand the different kinds of reading you need to be doing as a student
- use the advanced reading skills of deconstruction to analyse and evaluate texts
- recognise arguments, and show the difference between arguments and other kinds of writing
- make judgements about sources based on where they have come from and who has written them
- analyse and evaluate the structure of argument used in sources
- deconstruct the evidence used by sources to support their arguments.

This chapter will support you with the written examination paper, but also contains core skills which are needed for the essay, team project and your research report.

As you will remember, deconstruction is the first stage of the Critical Path, described in Chapter 1:

Deconstruction	→	Reconstruction	→	Reflection

Communication and Collaboration

Deconstruction

Introduction

This chapter is really about reading. As a student of Global Perspectives & Research, and of A Levels in general, you will need to develop some advanced reading skills. You may well think that you already know how to read effectively, and in fact in order to have reached this level of education you will not only have had to learn how to read, you will have had to establish and develop a good level of reading competence. In this chapter, you will be discovering that you still have plenty of opportunities to develop as a reader, and that it is possible to read in a number of different ways, for a variety of different purposes. Once you have done that, you will be able to practise in detail the reading skills required for effective deconstruction.

2.01 Advanced reading skills

KEY TERM

decoding: reading texts by mapping the marks on the page to specific meanings. Revealing the meaning is like breaking a code.

When you were first taught to read, you had to master the skill of **decoding**. Just as when you learnt to speak your native language, and had to connect the sounds you heard and made to specific meanings, when you learnt to read you had to link marks on the page to the specific word they represented, and the meaning of that word. Reading sentences, paragraphs and then longer texts was a matter of linking together those marks on the page with longer and more substantial chains of meaning. As the texts become longer and the range and type of vocabulary more challenging, this is a more demanding process, one all of us are still engaged with for the whole of our lives. The texts you are reading now, especially for your A Level subjects, require significantly more of you than those you read when you were younger. A lot of the reading you do for pleasure, like magazines or social media updates, or encounter in your everyday life, such as street signs or bus timetables, makes fewer demands, but the process of decoding is still the same.

ACTIVITY 2.01

Make a list in a journal of everything you read over the course of one day. This would include everything from street signs, printed instructions and web pages to writing in a textbook or on a whiteboard.

Look back at what you have written, and conclude your journal entry with a short paragraph reflecting on your reading for the day. Were you surprised by its amount or variety?

ACTIVITY 2.02

Decode this text so that you are clear about what each word and sentence means. When you have done this you should be able to answer the two questions which follow.

Internet, a system architecture that has revolutionized communications and methods of commerce by allowing various computer networks around the world to interconnect. Sometimes referred to as a "network of networks," the internet emerged in the United States in the 1970s but did not become visible to the general public until the early 1990s. . . .

From the entry for 'internet' in the Encyclopædia Britannica

1 Why is the internet sometimes known as a 'network of networks'?
2 When were the general public first aware of the internet?

Discussion point

Discuss with at least one other student how you went about doing this activity. How did decoding the text help you, and were there things that just decoding prevented you from doing?

Active reading

One of the most important lessons you need to learn as a student is that you are an active participant in your own reading. The texts you read are not just units of knowledge to be passively absorbed. Instead, you have a role to play as a reader in not only decoding the text, but taking it apart more thoroughly. This means asking questions and making judgements about what you are reading.

ACTIVITY 2.03

Read the following short text:

Even though the internet is now an established part of the modern world, there remains much debate about its benefits and drawbacks. On the one hand, the internet connects people and organisations, and makes the flow of ideas and information much more efficient than it has been in the past. On the other hand, that ease of communication can be a drawback, as it is more difficult to maintain personal privacy as a result.

1   What are the advantages and disadvantages of the internet according to this text?

2   Do you think the internet's benefits outweigh its drawbacks or not? Explain your answer.

Reflection:

- How did your approach to the text differ when answering the questions in Activity 2.02 and 2.03?

- What does this tell us about what is involved in active reading?

In order to actively engage with the text in Activity 2.03, you would have had to identify the debate, and separately group the advantages and disadvantages. In order to answer the final question in the activity, you would also have had to make judgements about how convincing each side was, and compare your own views with those in the text. Because of this, your reading did not simply involve decoding but also required analysis and evaluation: actively breaking down the text into smaller parts, and using that to make judgements about what it said.

2.02 What is an argument?

We have already seen in this chapter that there are different ways of reading. There are also different kinds of text. We can see this if we return to the topic of the impact of the internet.

Deconstruction

ACTIVITY 2.04

Compare these three sentences:

A: The internet is a series of interconnecting computer networks.

B: The internet connects people, therefore it is a good thing.

C: The internet is a bad thing because when we use it we are forced to share information about ourselves with others.

List the ways in which these sentences are the same, and the ways in which they differ from one another.

KEY TERMS

claim: a statement which may or may not be true

reason: a claim used to support a conclusion

assertion: an unsupported claim

conclusion: a claim about the world which we are asked to accept based on reasons

argument: one or more reasons leading to a conclusion

argument indicator: a term used specifically to signpost the reasons or conclusions in an argument

Reflection: Sentence A is a purely descriptive statement: it tells us what the internet is. Sentences B and C, however, begin with **claims**, statements which express a view about the internet with which people might agree or disagree. In fact, these two sentences illustrate this perfectly, as the two claims directly contradict each other:

The internet is a good thing.

The internet is a bad thing.

Because of this, when we present claims, we also need to provide **reasons** to go with our claims to justify why other people should accept them. Otherwise, our claims are just **assertions**: statements about things which only repeat our own opinions without any justification. Once a claim has at least one reason to go with it, then it is a **conclusion**, as it provides a justification for us to accept something with which others might disagree. Both B and C do this, as follows:

Conclusion B: the internet is a good thing
Reason B: it connects people

Conclusion C: the internet is a bad thing
Reason C: it forces us to share information about ourselves with others

In both cases, the combination of a conclusion with at least one reason makes it an **argument**. Both use processes of rational thought to ask us to accept something. Sometimes arguments use specific words to connect their reasons to their conclusion. We can see this as example B in the original sentence uses the word *therefore*. This indicates that what comes after the word is the conclusion, and what comes before are the reasons. The word *because* in example A has a similar purpose, except here the word indicates that what comes before is the conclusion, and what comes afterwards are the reasons. Both *therefore* and *because* are examples of **argument indicators,** as they are terms which indicate, or point out, the different parts of an argument. As we have also seen, however, these are not required to make something an argument: all this needs is at least one reason and one conclusion which are linked to one another. Using indicators as signposts just makes it clearer.

Arguments and disputes

There are also other meanings for the word 'argument', however. This is an argument too:

Person 1: I love the internet.
Person 2: I hate it. It's the worst thing ever.

This meaning of argument, as a dispute between people, is probably more familiar to you. Again, we have a difference of opinion, but each side relies on assertion, and emotions probably also have a big part to play.

When we follow the Critical Path, we will certainly be interested in exploring and making decisions about variations of opinion between opposing groups of people. However, the crucial difference is that we will want each side to justify itself using arguments in the other sense, with reasons leading to conclusions.

Discussion point

- Discuss with other students what you understand by the term 'argument'.
- Which type of argument do you find more useful: a dispute, or reasons leading to conclusions? Does it depend on the circumstances in which you find yourself?

Recognising arguments

One important skill you will need when finding arguments to support your research is to be able to recognise them when you come across them, and also to know the difference between arguments and other kinds of writing.

As we have just seen, arguments in our sense can only be reasons that lead to a conclusion. As we have seen, the conclusion is often signposted by an argument indicator, like the word 'therefore'. However, other words, such as 'because', might be used to indicate conclusions or – most often – there is no argument indicator at all, but the conclusion is still present. This still means, however, that we can use a helpful technique called the **therefore test** when looking for arguments to work out whether we have found one.

KEY TERM

therefore test: a technique which inserts the word *therefore* into a text to test whether or not it is an argument

The therefore test works by inserting the word *therefore* immediately to the left of what you think is the conclusion to the argument. If it really is an argument, you should then be able to insert reasons from the argument before the word *therefore* in a way that makes sense, so you can see that the reasons lead to the conclusion.

Take the following example:

> It is important to use content filtering to restrict access to the internet. A lot of material which is available online is inappropriate for children.

We might identify the first sentence of this argument as the conclusion. We can confirm this using the therefore test:

> A lot of material which is available online is inappropriate for children, **therefore** it is important to use content filtering to restrict access to the internet.

Deconstruction

Try using the therefore test with these extracts to work out which of them are arguments and which are not.

1   During my lifetime I have dedicated my life to this struggle of the African people. I have fought against white domination, and I have fought against black domination. I have cherished the ideal of a democratic and free society in which all persons will live together in harmony and with equal opportunities. It is an ideal for which I hope to live for and to see realised. But, My Lord, if it needs be, it is an ideal for which I am prepared to die.

From Nelson Mandela's statement from the dock at the opening of the defence case in the Rivonia trial, 20 April 1964

2   Nelson Mandela was one of the most significant world figures of the 20th century. This is because he served as the first black President of South Africa. He was also highly influential as a global symbol of opposition to the system of Apartheid (racial segregation) in that country. Finally, he is also famous for supporting non-violent opposition to Apartheid despite spending many years in prison.

3   Nelson Mandela was President of South Africa from 1994 to 1999. He was born in 1918 and worked as a lawyer before joining the African National Congress and campaigning against the system of Apartheid in South Africa. He was held in prison for 27 years until 1990.

You may find the following commentary helpful in checking and discussing your answers:

Extract 1 seems very convincing in its insistence on the importance and fairness of the struggle in which Nelson Mandela was involved when he was on trial in 1964. However, wherever we insert the word *therefore*, we cannot highlight a clear conclusion supported by reasons. In fact, it repeats the words 'domination' and 'ideal' and uses two contrasting pairs of words – 'white' and 'black' and 'live' and 'die' to make what it is asserting about that struggle emotionally convincing. This is, in fact, an example of **rhetoric**, language designed to be persuasive, rather than argument, which is language structured to rationally support its conclusions with reasons. We can certainly admire it, and even analyse and evaluate how it achieves its effects, but it is not part of the Critical Path.

Extract 2 is an argument about Nelson Mandela. You may even have spotted the alternative argument indicator, *because*. We can also, however, demonstrate it is an argument by using the therefore test:

- he served as the first black President of South Africa
- he was highly influential as a global symbol of opposition to the system of Apartheid
- he is famous for supporting non-violent opposition to Apartheid despite spending many years in prison
- **therefore** Nelson Mandela was one of the most significant world figures of the 20th century

You may not agree that Mandela was one of the most significant world figures of the 20th century, and you do not have to. However, it is demonstrable that this is an argument which tries to make the case that he was.

Extract 3 is not an argument: it is simply a series of descriptive statements about Mandela, and inserting the word *therefore* anywhere does not allow us to distinguish any reasons or conclusions.

KEY TERM

rhetoric: language which is primarily designed to persuade its reader or listener, rather than using rational techniques of argument to demonstrate the strength of the case it wishes to make

Discussion point

Use what you have learnt in this section to share with other students or your teacher examples of arguments, rhetoric or descriptions you have come across in your other subjects or more generally.

2.03 Evaluating arguments

Once we have identified a range of arguments responding to an issue, we need to evaluate them. As we saw in Chapter 1 when introducing this term, evaluation measures the strengths and weaknesses of something in order to make a judgement about its value.

Identification and evaluation work together as essential stages in the active reading of sources. Recognising this and putting it into practice is an important stage of your development as a student of Global Perspectives.

Up until this point in this chapter, we have focused on recognising arguments, and **identifying** where the parts of the argument (the conclusion and reasons) can be found in a source. This might also involve **explaining** how the reasons are linked to the conclusion, and why the conclusion is what it is.

Evaluation relies on identification and explanation – we need to know what we are assessing and pick out its strengths and weaknesses before we can make that judgement about its value or acceptability. This is why terms like 'assess' or questions like 'to what extent' or 'how convincing' are often used as equivalents to 'evaluate': they refer to the same process of weighing up and making judgements about parts of an argument.

Your ability to apply these skills when you read a text are directly tested in the written paper, but they are also skills you will need when reading any text throughout the course, so it is important to establish them at the start.

Deconstruction, as the first stage of the Critical Path, is concerned with identifying parts of arguments and explaining how they work in order to make decisions about which arguments are stronger and which are weaker. Knowing this will help in reflecting on the larger judgements required by the later stages of the path.

There are several separate, specific ways in which arguments we find as sources can be measured:

1 the **structure** of the argument: how closely reasons relate to conclusions and how effectively different lines of argument support one another

2 the **evidence** supporting the argument: the quantity, type and quality of pieces of evidence used to back up individual reasons

3 the **context** of the argument: who wrote it, where it was published, when it was written

The following sections of this chapter focus on each of these in turn, showing how they represent different ways of reading arguments. We will then see how they can be combined in order to fully evaluate, or deconstruct, sources, including weighing them up against one another.

KEY TERMS

identify: to establish what or where something is in a text

explain: to show understanding of something in a text by describing it in additional detail

KEY TERMS

structure: the organisation of a text, and how each element within it is placed together

evidence: facts or other data supporting reasons or claims

context: factors that are outside the source and its argument, such as its author or where it was published, that affect its meaning

Deconstruction

2.04 Evaluating the structure of arguments

When exploring art in an international context, one popular area of debate concerns the status of graffiti, images or text placed on walls in public areas which, usually, do not have the permission of the property owner. This short extract from an argument by Heather MacDonald, published in *The New York Times*, is an example of an argument which is frequently made against graffiti:

Graffiti is always vandalism. By definition it is committed without permission on another person's property, in an adolescent display of entitlement. Whether particular viewers find any given piece of graffiti artistically compelling is irrelevant. Graffiti's most salient characteristic is that it is a crime.

MacDonald, H. (2014) 'Graffitti is always vandalism', The New York Times *(11 July 2014).*

This argument consists of a conclusion and three reasons. We could place them in list form as follows:

- *Conclusion:* Graffiti is always vandalism
- *Reason 1:* The definition of graffiti is that it is placed on someone else's property without permission
- *Reason 2:* It is not relevant if specific individuals see graffiti as art
- *Reason 3:* The most important characteristic of graffiti is that it is a crime

KEY TERMS

strength: a feature of an argument which makes it more likely it will be accepted

weakness: a feature of an argument which makes it less likely it will be accepted

line of argument: a separate direction or type of argument which leads to the conclusion

counter-argument: an argument which could be made to challenge another argument

inferential gap: the gap of reasoning between a reason and the conclusion it supports

assumption: an unstated reason which needs to be included in order for an argument to work successfully

When evaluating this argument in terms of its structure, we need to take note of its **strengths** and **weaknesses**. One strength here is that it has more than one **line of argument**. This means that the three reasons each independently support the conclusion from different directions. Reason 1 claims that graffiti shares part of its definition with the definition of vandalism: both involve doing something to someone else's property without permission. Reason 2 claims that just because some people say that graffiti is art does not mean that it is not actually vandalism. Finally, Reason 3 says that even if it has other characteristics, the most important characteristic of graffiti is that it is a crime. Each of these lines of argument takes a different potential **counter-argument**, or argument against the conclusion, and challenges it.

Another area for evaluation, however, is how closely connected each reason is to the conclusion. We call this the **inferential gap**, and it can be represented visually with Reason 2:

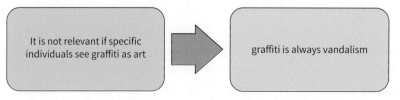

In order to accept the conclusion on the basis of this reason, we would need to insert some other claims into the gap. The first is that the majority of people see graffiti as vandalism. The second might be that, in this case, the opinion of the majority is always more important than that of the minority.

We can call these unstated claims **assumptions**: reasons which are not explicitly included in the argument but which must be placed there in order to accept that the conclusion follows from the reasons which are stated. The more assumptions which need to be made in order to accept the conclusion, however, the weaker the argument can be said to be.

Graffiti Is Young, Cool, Creative – Let It Happen

If graffiti is inspiring, it's because it's fun, cool and does not take formal training. Young kids who paint on the walls are screaming to be heard and, yes, we all started that way. My husband and I have to clean graffiti off of my property from time to time, but I see it as the price we all pay for urban living. A bit of rebellion is something we should champion as a society. Somebody has to question the status quo – or we'll grow stagnant.

I, for one, would also rather see the creative outpouring of our youth on the walls instead of the billboards and advertising inflicted upon us around every corner. The art world has already acknowledged the value of it. Street art has become wildly marketable.

By encouraging kids to create art in this medium – and not just tag their names across walls – we could empower generations. Who knows? They might even be able to make a living doing what they love.

Pink, L. (2014) 'Graffiti Is Young, Cool, Creative – Let It Happen', The New York Times (11 July 2014).

Reflection: The conclusion of this article is contained in the headline: we are being asked to 'let it happen'. Applying the therefore test, the three reasons leading directly to this conclusion are firstly that it is 'young', secondly that it is 'cool' and thirdly that it is 'creative'. Each of these in turn is supported by separate lines of argument in the body of the article.

As we weigh up strengths and weaknesses, we could note that it is strengthened in its support by three distinct lines of reasoning. It also acknowledges a counter-argument, that people have to clear graffiti off their property, but responds to it as the price we pay for urban living.

The most significant potential weakness in this argument is the number of substantial inferential gaps. For example, the claim that graffiti is creative is supported by the further claim that its creativity is preferable to billboard advertising. Between the two steps is an inferential gap which would need to be filled with the assumption that graffiti is more creative than advertising. Why this should be is not clear: is it because youthfulness is assumed to be equivalent to creativity, or is there another argument which says that art produced by corporations cannot be creative? Part of the problem is that the word 'creative' itself is not clearly defined, nor is the word 'cool'. The importance of defining terms as part of making arguments is addressed in Chapter 3.

Comparing strengths and weaknesses and making evaluative judgements

Evaluating the structure of arguments, like the other aspects of arguments, requires using the strengths and weaknesses we have identified to make a judgement on how acceptable they are overall. In the case of each of these arguments about graffiti, this judgement is likely to depend on whether one accepts the assumptions it requires. MacDonald's reasoning against graffiti requires us to accept that the majority view on the issue will be correct because most people hold it. Pink, on the other hand, requires us to prioritise youth and change above the majority status quo. Which of the two you decide to support is dependent, in this case, on which set of assumptions you prefer.

To summarise, when we are evaluating arguments based on their structure, we are judging how well constructed they are, as if we were trying to decide if a house was built well or not. This is based on two factors:

- how extensive the foundations are: is there a range of lines of argument, how well do they support each other, and how effectively do they address each aspect of the conclusion?
- how large the gaps in the fabric of the building are: are there excessively large inferential gaps between stages of reasoning which require the insertion of assumptions as missing reasons, or perhaps as an overall claim to make the argument work?

Just because there are gaps to fill does not necessarily mean that we will make an evaluative judgement that the argument overall is less convincing. What may matter most is whether we agree with the assumptions which would need to be used to fill those gaps: if we cannot, then the argument as a whole is more likely to be rejected; if we can, then that may make it more likely we will accept it.

More complex structures of argument

Before moving on from argument structure, we can read one more argument about graffiti, this time by Lu Olivero, director of the Aerosol Carioca, a group based in Rio de Janeiro which focuses on the academic study of graffiti. It appeared in the same special feature in *The New York Times* as the previous two arguments:

Graffiti straddles the line between pure art and pure vandalism.

Banksy's work has unintentionally reignited the "art or vandalism" debate: though the British government has been vigilant in removing his trademark stencil art, labeling it "vandalism," his original works and knockoffs have skyrocketed in price over the last decade. His work is often highly satirical of establishment rules and politics. Why is it that Banksy's work is gobbled up by the same people he is critical of – yet his contemporaries are looked at as "criminals"? Why are they judged so differently?

Thirty years ago hip-hop music was labeled "noise," and graffiti will follow the same trajectory. *Perceptions about street art have already drastically changed.*

For example, in Brazil, during late 1990s, it was common for graffiti artists to be harassed or shot at by the police. Today, many of the same officers support graffiti initiatives for city beautification, and as a crime deterrent. They understand that graffiti can be a career opportunity for youth in low-income neighborhoods. The growth of graffiti in Brazil, and its role in challenging the status quo, demonstrates the power of art, and its ability to create dialogue.

> *The truth is that despite the acceptance of graffiti, it needs the law so that it can function outside of it.* This is where innovation is born, and this is what pushes the art to evolve. Had graffiti artists in Brazil painted inside the lines of the law, many internationally acclaimed artists would never have existed.
>
> Olivero, L. (2014) 'Graffiti Is a Public Good, Even As It Challenges the Law', *The New York Times (11 July 2014).*

ACTIVITY 2.07

Can you come up with a key for labelling each of the coloured sections of this argument (**red**, **blue**, green and **orange**)? Each relates to the structure of the argument.

Reflection: The text in red is perhaps the easiest to label. It is the conclusion of Olivero's argument. We can confirm this by using the therefore test, as the claims made in the rest of the argument all support this as a conclusion: graffiti lies between art and vandalism. Yet the rest of the argument is longer than the previous examples we have looked at, and not all of it has been reproduced here. Not only this, it seems to fall into several dissimilar sections. The text in blue is concerned with the British street artist Banksy; the section in green is about how perceptions of street art have changed, especially in Brazil; the orange section is about the relationship between graffiti in general and the law.

We can use what we have learnt already to call these lines of argument: each is a separate pillar supporting the final conclusion from a different direction. But these lines of argument are much more substantial than the ones we have previously looked at. Each works as an argument in itself. We can tell this because the sentence in italics within each section works as a conclusion just for that section, and the therefore test can be used to show that. For example, the fact that Banksy's art has been removed consistently by the authorities, combined with the reason that it has massively increased in value in the art market, leads to the conclusion that his work has reignited the debate about the status of graffiti between vandalism and art.

We can call this sort of conclusion an **intermediate conclusion**, as it is not the final conclusion of the argument. That is called the **main conclusion**. Instead it works as a reason which supports the main conclusion, but also clearly organises each line of argument. Out in the real world, as an active reader, you are more likely to encounter longer and more complex arguments such as this. Therefore, a key skill of reading is to be able to break these arguments down into the smaller arguments which make them up. This type of navigation will help you to extract the precise sections of argument you need in order to be able to reconstruct and reflect on debates effectively yourself.

2.05 Evaluating the evidence supporting an argument

The structure of the argument itself is not the only aspect we need to consider when evaluating its effectiveness. The evidence supporting each reason or line of argument is equally important. By 'evidence' we mean the facts or other kinds of information which back

KEY TERMS

intermediate conclusion: a conclusion which also functions as a reason leading to the main conclusion. It is supported by reasons within a specific section of an argument.

main conclusion: the final conclusion of an argument

up claims or reasons. As well as evaluating the argument itself, we can also weigh up each piece of evidence when coming to an overall judgement.

Types of evidence

Evidence can come in a number of different types. One of the main distinctions is between **primary evidence** and **secondary evidence**.

Primary evidence can be thought of as the raw material from which we can know about something. It can be a first-hand account, produced by someone who has witnessed an event, or it might be measurements taken directly of the thing being described.

Secondary evidence, on the other hand, consists of books or articles which have been based on the primary evidence. They might summarise the primary evidence for us, or draw together different sources of evidence for something, but the ability to do this means that the secondary evidence will always be placed between us and the primary evidence for an event or situation.

Other types of evidence are **quantitative evidence** which describes things numerically, and **qualitative evidence** which instead describes things subjectively, or in other ways which cannot be reduced to numerical data.

Evidence can also consist of **facts** or **opinions**. Facts can be checked against other sources of evidence, and remain the same: someone's height, for example, or the volume of carbon monoxide generated by the traffic in a city. Opinions depend on individuals' judgement of the value of something, and are based solely on their own point of view. An opinion cannot be questioned on its own terms, but can only be challenged by another, different opinion on the same matter. For example, one opinion, or value judgement, about motor vehicles is that they imprison us in congested cities. Another is that they free people to move around and between geographical areas in ways that would not have previously been possible.

Questions about evidence

As we have seen, the variety of different kinds of evidence means that we cannot make straightforward judgements about a piece of evidence simply based on its type. Primary evidence is not always better than secondary evidence, and opinions can sometimes – but not always – be more effective than facts. Instead it is more important to ask questions about the evidence we encounter in arguments to help us make decisions about its **reliability**: whether we accept that it provides sufficient support for the claim in the argument to which it is being attached.

Asking questions is one of the most important dispositions, or kinds of behaviour, we can have when following the Critical Path, and applies particularly to the active reading which is required by deconstruction.

Is it relevant?

The first key question to ask about any piece of evidence is whether it is relevant to the claim it is being used to support. This is illustrated in the following article, published in *The Guardian* newspaper in the UK in 2013, by Chris Faulkner, CEO of Breitling Energy Corporation, which specialises in 'fracking', the injection of high-pressure liquid into underground rock to release deposits of gas.

KEY TERMS

primary evidence: first-hand information, directly about something

secondary evidence: evidence combined or summarised from primary evidence, but not directly from the situation itself

quantitative evidence: evidence which measures the amount of something, usually numerically

qualitative evidence: evidence which measures the quality of something as attributes which cannot be summarised as numerical quantities

facts: measurements of things which are accepted to actually exist, and which can be proved or disproved

opinion: an individual's judgement of the value of something. These cannot be proved or disproved, but can be challenged by other opinions.

KEY TERM

reliability: the extent to which a piece of evidence provides acceptable support for a claim or reason

Why the UK should embrace fracking

The United Kingdom is braced for the worst winter in 60 years, with heavy snows and record cold forecast. For many, survival will take a huge toll on the handbag: last year, the average fuel bill soared to a record £1,353, and the Office for Budget Responsibility says it will increase by £100 on average this year.

If that does not make you shiver, consider this: at one point last winter, the UK's gas supply was a mere six hours from empty.

It does not have to be that way. The future will be a lot warmer if the UK can muster the political will to look to a promising new alternative in energy production – hydraulic fracturing, or "fracking", a drilling technique that releases natural gas stuck in shale formations, opening access to enormous underground reserves.

So far, the UK has refrained from taking advantage of this extraordinary ability to tap previously inaccessible reserves, citing environmental concerns. A close look at the fracking experience across the Atlantic, however, demonstrates how unfounded the concerns are and how beneficial fracking can be, both environmentally and economically.

As the United States has become more adept at tapping its existing energy resources, largely through fracking, the yields have been astronomical: this year, the US became the biggest natural gas producer in the world.

. . .

Faulkner, C. (2013) 'Why the UK should embrace fracking', The Guardian.

As the article's headline suggests, it concludes that the UK should embrace fracking. The evidence it uses to support this could be set out as follows:

1 The UK is forecast to have the worst winter in 60 years
2 The average UK fuel bill went up to £1353 last year
3 This year it will increase by £100
4 Last winter, at one point, the UK was six hours away from running out of gas
5 The US has become the biggest global natural gas producer in the world using fracking

ACTIVITY 2.08

Take the opportunity to ask some questions, as an individual or in groups, about the relevance of the evidence used by Chris Faulkner in his argument. How relevant is each piece of evidence to his conclusion, that the UK should embrace fracking?

Once you have written out your ideas about each piece of evidence, read the reflection below which discusses some ideas about how the relevance of this evidence can be evaluated.

> **Reflection:** The first piece of evidence is about the weather in the UK, and is of a forecast, a piece of secondary evidence, as it is an analysis of data about the weather. It does not seem to be directly relevant to fracking. The next two pieces of evidence relate to domestic energy costs in the UK: their level and rate of increase. Again, this does not seem directly relevant to fracking as a method of energy generation.
>
> The fourth piece of evidence is more relevant, as it is at least evidence of levels of gas reserves in the UK, and the source tells us that fracking is a method of gas extraction. It is not the only method, however, so this piece of evidence would not exclusively support fracking.

The final piece of evidence is not from the UK at all, but from the USA, and is evidence of the economic success enjoyed by the US through fracking as the biggest natural gas producer in the world. It is the most relevant piece of evidence, as it is the only one that describes the benefits of fracking directly. It comes from a different country, however, and requires us to draw the conclusion: in this case adding an intermediate conclusion, which is not supplied in the argument, that the UK will enjoy economic success from fracking. This in turn becomes a reason supporting the conclusion that the UK should embrace fracking.

As can be seen from this reflection, evidence can have differing degrees of relevance to the conclusion being drawn. When evaluating the relevance of evidence as part of an overall argument, we therefore need to ask some important questions:

1   Where is this evidence relevant to the claim being made, and the overall conclusion of the argument? Where is it irrelevant?

2   What further assumptions, evidence or claims would be required to make the evidence relevant to the conclusion?

3   Overall, can we accept the conclusion on the basis of the relevance of the evidence which supports it?

Is it significant or selective?

The final set of questions we should be able to ask about evidence is whether it is selective or significant. Like relevance, these are concerned with which evidence the writer of the argument has chosen to use, and how well it supports their conclusion.

If evidence is **selective** then the argument includes some evidence but leaves other evidence out in order to more strongly support its own conclusion. Although the evidence which is included can be said to be therefore more sharply focused, it is also a negative strategy in that the evidence which is excluded has the potential to challenge the conclusion which has been reached.

The **significance** of evidence, on the other hand, is a measure of whether the writer of the argument has chosen the best possible evidence that provides the fullest support for their argument. Is the evidence that has been used significant, or meaningful, in supporting the argument?

As with our previous reading questions, the best means of understanding them is to see them used in evaluating an actual argument. This is an article on the website of Greenpeace USA, a campaigning environmental charity:

The Dangers of Fracking

Since 2005, more than 100,000 oil and gas wells have been drilled and fracked in the United States.

Fracking has been pursued by countries like Canada, India, the U.K., and China, and in numerous U.S. states.

. . .

Fracking is a water-intensive process. In water-scarce Western states like Texas and Colorado, more than 3.6 million gallons of water are used every time a well is fracked, which can happen multiple times throughout the life of a well.

The process involves injecting a huge quantity of fresh water mixed with toxic chemicals—called fracking fluids—deep into the ground. Fossil fuels companies routinely claim that these fracking fluids are harmless because they're roughly 2 percent chemical and 98 percent water. But 2 percent of the billions of gallons of fracking fluid created by drillers every year equals hundreds of tons of toxic chemicals, many of which are kept secret by the industry.

. . .

While the fossil fuel industry denies it, the EPA has acknowledged the connection between fracking and increased earthquakes since 1990.

Scientists have made firm links between earthquakes in Colorado, Oklahoma, Ohio and Arkansas in the past few years.

Oklahoma, for example, averaged 21 earthquakes per year above a 3.0 magnitude between 1967 and 2000. Since 2010 and the beginning of the fracking boom, the state has averaged more than 300 earthquakes above 3.0 magnitude every year.

. . .

Fracking is diverting money and attention from the real long-term solutions we need for a sustainable energy system, while adding to greenhouse gas pollution and environmental degradation.

→

Deconstruction

> Join us in telling government and big business to stop pursuing this false solution and start focusing on the energy future we want, one based on clean and renewable energy.
>
> *Greenpeace USA, 'Fracking'. Available from: http://www.greenpeace.org/usa/global-warming/ issues/fracking/, n.d.*

ACTIVITY 2.09

This article concludes that governments and corporations should stop fracking and turn to alternative sources of energy.

1 List the pieces of evidence used in the Greenpeace USA article.

2 For each piece of evidence you list, identify the claim in the article it is being used to support, and consider how well it supports the main conclusion.

3 Reflect on what you have found:

   a What is the most significant evidence that supports the conclusion? Is any of the evidence less significant?

   b Is the evidence used here at all selective? Why?

Reflection: The article uses a number of different items of evidence. For example:

- the 100,000 oil wells drilled and fracked in the United States
- the 3.6 million gallons of water used each time a well is fracked
- the increased earthquakes in Oklahoma since 2010

Some of the evidence is both relevant to the conclusion and significant in supporting it. The water used by fracking, especially as this is located in states which are susceptible to drought, supports the conclusion that fracking should be stopped because of its environmental impact.

Some pieces of evidence are less firmly significant, however. The number of wells drilled and the list of countries involved are not linked to claims at all. This might support the conclusion that fracking is now a widespread activity, but not in itself that it should be stopped.

The shift in Oklahoma's average number of earthquakes from 21 per year to over 300 since 2010, when fracking started to be increasingly employed, seems convincing. Yet this is selective: we do not have information about earthquake frequencies in other areas at the same time, or any other factors apart from fracking which might have led to the earthquakes. We would need more evidence from other sources in order to be able to accept the link. This is called **corroboration**: evidence used from one source to confirm the acceptability of another.

Comparative evaluation of evidence

Both of these sources, Chris Faulkner's case for fracking, and Greenpeace USA's argument against, use a range of evidence to support their claims. This means that although we have identified some weaknesses in evaluating them individually, neither is obviously weaker than the other overall, although they are quite different in the way that they support their conclusions.

When locating and reading sources in order to explore debates around Global Perspectives & Research issues, it is not useful to seek out obviously weak evidence and demonstrate its shortcomings. This does not tell us very much about the merits of each side. Instead, analysing the different kinds of evidence each source offers will better enable us to make a decision between them.

ACTIVITY 2.10

Compare the examples of evidence from Faulkner and Greenpeace USA in the table below:

Faulker	Greenpeace USA
UK fuel bill £1353	3.6 million gallons water used
US will be biggest natural gas producer	earthquakes increased to over 300 per annum

Table 2.01: The fracking debate: evidence presented by Faulkner and by Greenpeace USA

1 What other items of evidence could you add from the sources to each column of the table?

2 Look at the type of evidence from each article. What differences do you notice and does this help you to make a decision?

Discussion point

You may have noticed in Activity 2.10 that the evidence from Chris Faulkner of Breitling Energy tended to be financial: about the economic benefits of fracking, or the economic disadvantages associated with not fracking. Greenpeace USA, on the other hand, uses evidence of the environmental impact of fracking to argue against it: the amount of water used, and earthquakes generated.

If you had to choose a side in the fracking debate based on the evidence presented, which one would it be and how would you decide? When you discuss this with others, you may find that some people identify that the case for fracking here comes from an economic point of view, because that is the nature of the evidence it presents, whereas the case against tends to be environmental. Therefore, it is no longer really a matter of which side presents the stronger or weaker evidence. Rather, it is a matter of whether we judge the strengths of economic evidence to be more or less significant than those of the environmental. Which do you value more, the economic or the environmental, and does this lead you towards judging on one side of the debate or the other?

2.06 Evaluating the context of arguments

When considering the context of arguments, we are not looking at the structure of the argument itself or its evidence, but at where it comes from. The word 'context' comes from the Latin verb *texere*, to 'weave together'. The prefix 'con' often means 'with' something else, so when we speak of context we mean what is woven together with the text: the people, organisations or environments outside the text of the argument itself which influence, control or organise its meanings. We often do not see these directly or obviously within the

Deconstruction

argument itself, but they can have a significant impact on the conclusions it reaches, the evidence it selects and the assumptions it makes.

There are two main ways in which an active reading, following the Critical Path, can make use of context. The first is to *exclude* arguments we may not want to use on either side of the debate when we are looking for suitable sources. We do this by evaluating a source's **credibility**: the factors in its context which might make its arguments more or less believable. By excluding less credible sources on both sides of the debate, we can ensure that we are comparing the strongest possible arguments when making a final judgement.

The second use of context is to help in *locating* arguments. Once we have ruled out weaker arguments and analysed the conclusions, lines of reasoning, assumptions and evidence of those which remain, the context of the source can help us to understand differences between them. Here, the purpose is not to be able to say which arguments are weaker and must be rejected, but instead to be able to choose which ones most convincingly line up with the position we want to choose for ourselves in our final judgement. Chapter 3, which combines the reconstruction, or comparison, of texts with deconstruction, and Chapter 4, which adds in reflection in a guide to planning and writing essays, explore these skills of selection, comparison and choice in much more detail. However, the skill of reading the context of texts will help with all of these.

> **KEY TERM**
>
> **credibility:** the believability of the claims made by a source related to its context

ACTIVITY 2.11

Make a list of the factors in the context of a source which might affect the credibility of its arguments or how we would respond to the judgements made by its conclusion. Examples of these might be the background of its writer or the date of publication.

Discussion point

You can extend the activity by reflecting individually or discussing with others what are the most useful or important contextual factors.

Assessing credibility

When a source is measured in terms of its credibility there are standard criteria, or standards of measurement, we can apply to do this. These are commonly listed as:

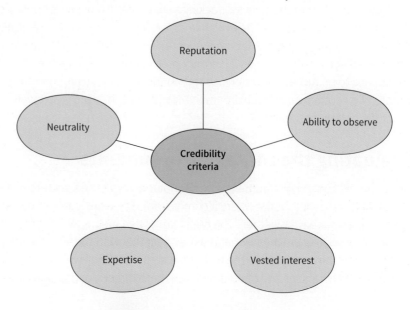

These criteria are most useful in helping us to prioritise the sources we might find most useful while undertaking research. Just as emergency personnel often undertake an initial assessment to identify the most urgent or serious cases before sending patients to hospital, credibility criteria are useful in performing an initial sorting of sources in order to identify which will provide the best support for each side of the debate.

The **reputation** of the writer or publication is the evidence we have that their claims, in general, are believable or reasonable. Reputations are built up over time, so a good way to evaluate the reputation of a source is to look at what else the writer has written and how it has been received by others, or how that publication has been written about previously. There are specific categories of publication summarised later in this section that can help us in making decisions about reputation.

Ability to observe is linked to the distinction we have already looked at between primary and secondary evidence. Sometimes a source may make claims about the situation itself, which is part of primary evidence, and we need to make a decision whether they were in a position to have observed that directly. For example, a newspaper reporter filing their report from London might make claims about a refugee camp in Iraq. If we know that they were not able to observe those conditions directly, then any eyewitness account might produce very large inferential gaps because of the assumptions involved. However, if their information is assembled from other, reliable sources of primary evidence, then the ability to observe becomes less important.

Sometimes a source might have a **vested interest** in the claims they are making. This means they would benefit directly from others' accepting the argument they are making. A multinational corporation might, for instance, argue for barriers to trade in a specific country to be lowered when they would then profit from that decision. Or, to use an example from earlier in the chapter, Breitling Energy Corporation has a vested interest in the UK's embracing fracking, as their business is based on gas extraction. However, just because they have a vested interest does not necessarily mean that fracking is a bad idea. It just means we have to be particularly careful in assessing their claims.

The **expertise** of a source is about knowledge they have which informs the case they make. This may enable them to select evidence and employ a level of detail which strengthens their arguments. For example, an environmental biologist would be able to draw on knowledge of ecological processes to closely argue about the consequences of pollution. However, this does not mean that university academics or professionals should always be believed just because of their background. The evidence they use and the arguments they make should be assessed on their own merits, especially if the context of the debate is different to their area of expertise. Experts are not experts about everything.

The degree of **neutrality** of a source refers to whether they have reason to select evidence in order to present a particular case. The argument from Greenpeace USA against fracking in Section 2.05 lacks neutrality because of its selection of exclusively environmental evidence in support of its case. Sometimes sources which are not neutral or balanced in their arguments are described as being **biased**, which is often seen as a weakness in itself. However, all arguments could be said to be biased because they select reasons and evidence in order to support their own conclusion and exclude counter-arguments which challenge them. This is why once a source has been selected, criticising it for bias in itself is a less helpful way of evaluating it.

KEY TERMS

reputation: the past actions or arguments made by a source which have an influence on their current credibility

ability to observe: how far a source has first-hand knowledge of the things it argues about

vested interest: the direct benefit a source would gain from having its conclusions accepted by others

KEY TERMS

expertise: the specific knowledge or learning a source has about the area in which it is arguing

neutrality: the degree to which a source either shows balance or deliberately selects argument and evidence in order to support a particular case

bias: a view of something which deliberately favours one particular aspect or opinion

ACTIVITY 2.12

The credibility criteria can be very helpful in categorising different kinds of source, and making judgements about whether the arguments they contain would be suitable for selection as the strongest representatives of each side of a debate.

Read the following three sources and comment on them using the five credibility criteria. How effective are they under each of these? Once you have done this, reflect on or discuss how this is related to the strengths and weaknesses of argument and evidence they show.

Source 1

Floody obvious

THE only certainty with Britain's weather is that, no matter what it does, it will be deemed proof of global warming.

A mild, rainy December with disastrous floods suits the climate change lobby. So would dry, bone-chilling cold.

But here's something more provably connected: our increasingly regular floods – and our rivers increasingly being too clogged with gravel and silt to drain water out to the sea.

That's because regular dredging is made almost impossible by a crazy EU law to keep rivers "natural" and protect the ecosystem. The result? Cities submerged. Lives and businesses ruined.

Dredging is not the only answer. But it would certainly provide more immediate protection than the puny efforts of climate change conferences to somehow turn down Earth's thermostat.

. . .

'The Sun Says' (2016), Floody obvious, The Sun (1 January 2016).

Source 2

Still hope on climate change

. . .

As most of the UK enjoys a brief August heatwave, Nasa has confirmed that July was the hottest month the world has experienced since records began. Even in Britain, where most of the month was wet and cool and felt not very summery at all, it was by a narrow margin the warmest month in the past 130 years of record-keeping – and it was the 10th month in a row that a new high was set. Siberian permafrost is melting, releasing lethal anthrax bacteria from thawing reindeer carcasses into the environment. There are floods in southern Louisiana which have killed 11 people and in California thousands are fleeing from forest fires. The link between short-term weather events and long-term changes in the climate may be tenuous, but it's just what the scientists warned about.

Ever since the general election . . . the political climate has seemed as bleak as the weather has been warm; subsidies for renewables have been cut and incentives intended to encourage landowners to give permission for fracking expanded. . . . Yet there are

→

glimmers of optimism, too. . . . The Paris climate summit commitment to cut carbon emissions far enough and fast enough to hold the rise in global temperatures below a maximum of 2C is helping to expand the market in renewables, not least by collapsing the appetite for investment in fossil fuels. . . .

The Guardian *(2016), 'The Guardian view on the heatwave: still hope on climate change' (17 August 2016).*

Source 3

Changing the climate debate

Discussion about climate change seems stuck in an unproductive dichotomy. One side argues vehemently that global warming is nothing but a grand hoax. The other side maintains that the planet is headed for catastrophe. In my book, *Cool It: The Skeptical Environmentalist's Guide to Global Warming*, I point out how neither side is right, and propose that we stake out a more sensible middle ground.

However, many people in this debate appear to identify almost tribally with one set of arguments. Kevin Watkins's review of my book is a case in point. He claims that while I don't deny that climate change is real, I understate the problems it causes.

. . .

Watkins is bothered by my reporting that the IPCC's estimates show that oceans will rise between 18–59cm, and that the most likely scenario is around 30cm. That's similar to what the planet experienced in the last 150 years and it (rather obviously) coped. Watkins also accuses me of being fixated on low estimates, yet I also consider the IPCC's projections of what would happen if Greenland were to melt much faster: sea levels would rise about 7cm and—at most—about 20cm.

Another complaint is that I encourage readers to "look on the bright side" of global warming. I submit that looking at both the negative and positive impacts of climate change is reasonable. Rising temperatures will mean more heat waves, but the cold is a much bigger killer than the heat. By 2050, global warming will cause almost 400,000 more heat-related deaths each year. Yet at the same time, 1.8m fewer people will die from cold. In this respect, global warming will save lives. Cooling our fears of global warming is important, because our panic often seems to affect our abilities to tackle the challenges of the 21st century. Yes, we need to fix global warming in the long run. But we are blindly focusing on policies that will not achieve this.

. . .

From Lomborg, B. (2007) 'Changing the Climate Debate', Prospect *magazine (25 November 2007).*

Deconstruction

Reflection: Undertaking this activity would first require some research on each of these publications. *The Sun* is a UK tabloid newspaper, with a reputation for courting popularity and focusing on entertainment alongside the reporting of news. *The Guardian*, on the other hand, is a broadsheet newspaper and seeks to maintain a reputation for accurate reporting of the news and well-informed argument, although it is still written and published for a mass audience. *Prospect*'s website describes itself as 'the leading magazine of ideas' and has a reputation for more intellectually demanding and specialised arguments in the field of politics, culture and economics.

Prospect's article is the only one with a named author: the others are issued under the authorship of the publication, so rely on their reputation in general. Bjorn Lomborg is described as adjunct professor at the Copenhagen Business School, part of the University of Copenhagen, and the author of *The Skeptical Environmentalist*, a book published by Cambridge University Press, giving this source the highest level of **expertise**. None of the sources have the ability to observe directly, but this seems less relevant in this case, as they are also making arguments using secondary evidence.

The **vested interest** of *The Guardian* and *Prospect* seems to be in maintaining their reputation, although in the case of *The Sun* this is less clear. Research into other editorial pieces from this publication would reveal other arguments which are hostile to the European Union, so there seems to be an interest in maintaining this position. None of the sources are **neutral**: Lomborg argues for a 'middle ground' on how worried we should be about global warming caused by humans. *The Guardian* argues firmly that climate change is a problem and we need to do something about it, while weighing up evidence for and against the case that effective action is taking place. *The Sun* shows least neutrality, and is tightly focused on its case that controlling carbon dioxide emissions is less effective than river dredging as a response to climate change.

These findings are also reflected in the arguments and evidence of the sources themselves. *The Sun* relies on assertions to support its conclusion and provides no evidence, whereas both *The Guardian* and Lomborg in *Prospect* support their arguments with evidence, although they reach opposing conclusions. From this it is these two sources which are most useful, and applying the criteria enables us to select them as the strongest representatives of different sides of this debate. But just because *The Sun* is a less credible source on this topic does not mean that scepticism about climate change caused by humans is necessarily a weaker argument: Lomborg's case demonstrates this. Instead, we need to locate and make sense of the differences and similarities between the strongest arguments we can find, organising them into perspectives. Doing this is the focus of Chapter 3.

Summary

In this chapter we have:

- reviewed the different kinds of reading that it is necessary to do as a student, and made a distinction between reading as decoding and active reading where we analyse and evaluate texts
- identified the skill of active reading as part of the first stage of the Critical Path, which is deconstruction
- defined arguments as conclusions supported by reasons and explored the differences between arguments and other types of text
- learnt how to evaluate the structure of arguments, including making judgements about how the conclusion is supported by lines of argument and the presence of assumptions and inferential gaps
- explored longer and more complex arguments where intermediate conclusions are present
- identified the different kinds of evidence used to support arguments
- developed a list of questions to ask about evidence in arguments in order to evaluate its strengths and weaknesses
- explored the implications of the context of arguments, especially their authorship
- evaluated the context of a range of sources containing arguments, applying credibility criteria.

It is important to recognise that we have been largely focusing on single sources in this chapter, learning to apply the tools of active reading, or deconstruction, to evaluate the structure of their arguments, their use of evidence and their context as sources. This is a useful starting point for the skills you need to develop as a Global Perspectives & Research student, and the longer question has given you the opportunity to practise them further.

The next stage will be to compare and group arguments more precisely into perspectives so that you can evaluate debates more broadly and reach conclusions. You will still be using the skills of deconstruction to weigh up arguments we have learnt in this chapter, but you will be aiming to make larger judgements about debates. This will be done individually, but also in collaboration with other students, and you will also learn how to communicate your findings in essays and presentations, rather than just in response to shorter questions.

Practising deconstruction

This section of the chapter is divided into three: firstly, developing deconstruction, secondly, establishing deconstruction and finally, enhancing deconstruction. Each section focuses on the active reading skill of deconstruction, but is also designed to build on the one before. You can either work through each section in turn or choose the section that you feel is at the most appropriate level for you. You should see a progression of difficulty through the three levels, but they are also linked in this chapter to the skills we have established at this stage of the Critical Path.

These sections use the topic of **Migration and Work**, one of the topics listed in the Cambridge International AS & A Level Global Perspectives & Research syllabus. However, you should be able to employ the principles of your learning here to a wide variety of other topics in the research you do and examination questions you answer.

Developing deconstruction

Read this source and answer the questions that follow.

Document 1

Here are the three biggest threats to the world right now

This article was published in *The Telegraph*, a UK newspaper, on 14 January 2016. Mehreen Khan is a business reporter. She writes on economics, the eurozone and global finance.

> Ahead of its annual meeting at Davos next week, the World Economic Forum has released its yearly assessment of the biggest dangers facing the world over the next decade.
>
> Large-scale migration is the global threat most likely to materialise over the next 18 months.
>
> More than 50pc of respondents said the involuntary mass movement of people seen over the last year would continue to be the chief source of instability in the world, over and above natural disasters and state conflict.
>
> Over 60 million refugees – equivalent to the population of the UK – were displaced from their homes last year alone, compared to just 40 million in the aftermath of the Second World War.
>
> . . .

1 Identify the conclusion of this argument.

2 Explain the two main reasons supporting this conclusion.

3 Identify the evidence that is used to support the conclusion.

4 Evaluate the strengths and weaknesses of the evidence in supporting the conclusion.

5 Assess the credibility of the writer.

6 Overall, how convincing do you find this argument?

Establishing deconstruction

Read this source and answer the questions that follow.

Document 2

> The world is undergoing a major population shift that will reshape economic development for decades.
>
> That's the view of the World Bank and the IMF. . . .
>
> "With the right set of policies, this era of demographic change can be an engine of economic growth," said World Bank group president, Jim Yong Kim. This presents an understandable challenge to politicians who tend not to think much further ahead than the next election, but the facts are stark. More than 90 per cent of global poverty is concentrated in low-income countries with a young population, while more than three-quarters of global growth is generated in richer nations with rising life expectancies. Against this backdrop, the movement of people becomes not just understandable, but predictable. In Sub-Saharan Africa, now suffering from a withdrawal of Chinese investment and fragile economies, the median age is just 18. Europe's focus might be on refugees, but the conditions facilitating a surge in economic migration are undeniable. Many identify Germany's openness to refugees as a response to its looming demographic pressures. By 2030, in EU countries, there will be around 2.5 people of working age for every pensioner. Faced with this reality, European nations would do well to heed the World Bank's advice that "freer cross-border flows of trade, investment, and people can help manage demographic imbalances". . . .
>
> Migration is now a fact of life . . . deal with it.
>
> This article was published in *City A.M.*, a UK newspaper, on 9 October 2015.

This document argues that there is a population shift from areas of global poverty which have low incomes and young populations to areas of global growth which are richer and have rising life expectancies.

1   Identify the reasons used to support this conclusion.

2   Identify the evidence used to support this conclusion.

3   Explain any assumptions which are required to accept the conclusion.

4   Evaluate the strengths and weaknesses of this argument.

Enhancing deconstruction

Write your own argument giving your view of migration. You should make sure you include:

• a conclusion

• reasons, with at least one line of argument

• evidence.

When you have finished, exchange your argument with someone else in your class, and evaluate the strengths and weaknesses of your arguments and evidence. You could also list the assumptions each of you has made.

Chapter 3
Deconstruction with reconstruction: organising sources and perspectives

Learning aims

By the end of this chapter, you should be able to:

- define what a perspective is
- appreciate the value of holding alternative perspectives
- compare the arguments in more than one source
- plan research into specific topics
- evaluate groups of sources
- identify and organise groups of sources around issues and debates.

This chapter will support you with the written examination paper and researching for writing essays, but also contains core skills which are needed for the team project and your research report.

Deconstruction	→	Reconstruction	→	Reflection
		Communication and Collaboration		

Introduction

Global Perspectives & Research links a process of learning to the world (because it is global) and to different ways of seeing the world (because it is about **perspectives**). Up until this point, we have been establishing and developing the skills of deconstruction: the active reading that allows us to identify, analyse and evaluate individual arguments on different topics.

However, as we saw in Chapter 1, that is not the end point of the Critical Path. Alongside the inward movement of deconstruction, we need the outward movement of reconstruction: combining, or synthesising, groups of sources. By identifying what sources have in common, or what makes them distinct, we can see where they are located, and the view of the world they have. It is only by doing this that we can get a sense of the bigger picture, and reflect in a secure and genuine way on what we think ourselves.

3.01 What are perspectives?

There is a traditional story, originating in the Indian subcontinent, of six blind men. They are told that an elephant has come to their village, but have no idea what this is, as they have never had the opportunity to see one. Instead, they decide to go to the elephant and to feel it. One touches the elephant's leg and declares that it is a pillar, another touches the tail and says it a rope. The third man feels the trunk and describes the elephant as a tree. The fourth, who touches the ear, says that it is a fan, whereas the fifth, feeling the belly, declares it is a wall. The final man, his fingers running along a tusk, describes the elephant as a solid pipe.

They argue and become annoyed with one another, each pointing to the part they had felt as evidence of what an elephant is. A wise man, in some versions of the story a king, then comes along and explains to them that they are all right: each described the elephant, but it became something different because of the part they had selected. Based on the evidence of the part they had felt, they had made a series of assumptions from other aspects of their experience and turned these into an argument for the elephant being something different.

> **KEY TERM**
>
> **perspective:** a coherent worldview which responds to an issue, made up of argument, evidence, assumptions, and perhaps also from a particular context

Deconstruction

Reconstruction

KEY TERMS

analogy: the use of one thing to explain or define something else

empathy: a fuller understanding of a perspective other than one's own, achieved by giving it sufficient space to be considered

We can use this story as an **analogy** for understanding perspectives in a global context. Analogies are comparisons made between one thing and another in order to better define or explain them. Although locating perspectives is not really the same as feeling the parts of an elephant, our use of them may have enough in common with how the elephant is understood in the story to make it a useful method of explanation. Ultimately, however, you will have to decide whether there are enough similarities between the two situations for the elephant story to be a usable analogy. If the differences are too numerous, its application may become misleading.

If we accept that there are some useful points of contact for now, then we can see the elephant as the world – everything that there is in our different global communities for us to think, feel and understand – and the parts felt by each person are separate perspectives upon it. Because we do not see the same evidence, we do not reach the same conclusions and sometimes do not even recognise the same world that we look at. Understanding this, however, is the first step to **empathy**, the capacity to recognise and give space to opinions about the world with which we do not agree.

ACTIVITY 3.01

Make a list of opinions you have with which you know other people disagree. If you are working in a group, then make a list of issues about which members of the group have different opinions. Examples of issues might include:

- whether students should be assessed by practical tasks, not written examinations
- whether nuclear power is an appropriate replacement for energy from fossil fuels
- whether it is right to test new medical treatments on animals to ensure the treatments are safe.

Without criticising others in the group, or trying to make them change their mind, write down the arguments and evidence that are used to justify each opinion.

- What do you notice about the similarities and differences between them?
- If the issue is your 'elephant', what part of its body would each of your opinions be? What does this tell us about perspectives?

Reflection: Just as the different individual parts of an elephant, when selected, can make the whole elephant appear as something completely different, opinions which come from different directions can make the issue appear rather differently. You may well have found that other people in your group relied on different reasons, evidence or even assumptions (unstated reasons) to yours and this led to a view of the issue which was unrecognisable to your own.

The anatomy of a perspective

Continuing to extend our analogy of the elephant and its parts, we can break down the parts of perspectives themselves by seeing them as bodies with different components to them. By mapping the anatomy, or bodily composition, or a perspective, we can acquire a better understanding of how it functions.

Perspectives are built from the following components, all of which we discussed in Chapter 2:

- reasons
- conclusions
- assumptions
- evidence
- context.

In other words, arguments from the same perspective may all share similar conclusions, or they might all employ lines of reasoning which are the same. Alternatively, they may have common assumptions, use the same or similar evidence or come from the same context as sources. It is also entirely possible that they might have more than one of these components in common.

We can see this even more clearly if we look at some examples of arguments.

ACTIVITY 3.02

Read the following two extracts from arguments about gender equality. Make a list of the differences and similarities between them.

Based on these, how would you summarise each perspective?

Extract 1: Achieving Gender Equality: When Everyone Wins

Gender equality is not only a fundamental human right but a necessary foundation for a peaceful, prosperous, and sustainable world. Providing women and girls with equal access to education, health care, decent work, and representation in political and economic decision-making processes will help create sustainable economies and benefit societies and humanity at large.

…

Over the last few decades, the world achieved considerable progress towards gender equality and women's empowerment. Many countries and societies moved forward, especially in the important field of education, where more girls are now enrolled in schools. Yet globally, women continue to face numerous challenges on issues ranging from gender based violence, economic, social and political participation, land inheritance and ownership, early marriage, and the possibility to work outside their homes.

Charlotta Sparre, Swedish Ambassador to Egypt, 'Achieving Gender Equality: When Everyone Wins' (2015), Daily News Egypt *(29 October 2015).*

Deconstruction

Reconstruction

Extract 2: Gender Equality

When guaranteed through equal opportunity, choice and access to resources, women's full participation in society and the economy multiplies the capacity of all for sustainable economic growth and social development.

Yet, despite regional advances to ensure gender equality and promote women's empowerment, women in Asia and the Pacific continue to face discriminatory policies, social and cultural barriers, and threats to their security that violate their rights and limit their potential.

…

United Nations Economic and Social Commission for Asia and the Pacific, 'Gender Equality', n.d.

Reflection: When comparing these two arguments, we can identify a number of points of similarity.

Conclusions and reasons

- Extract 1 concludes that 'gender equality is not only a fundamental human right but a necessary foundation for a peaceful, prosperous, and sustainable world' but also argues that 'women continue to face numerous challenges'.

- Extract 2 concludes that 'women's full participation in society and the economy multiplies the capacity of all for sustainable economic growth and social development' but also that 'women in Asia and the Pacific continue to face discriminatory policies'.

Assumptions

Both arguments assume that women's empowerment in itself will lead to sustainable social development and economic prosperity, and that there are no other alternative factors which would have a bigger impact on these.

Evidence

Apart from Extract 1's mention of the increase in girls enrolled in school, neither extract uses specific evidence in support of its claims.

Context

Extract 1 is by the Swedish Ambassador to Egypt. Extract 2 is by a UN agency working in Asia and the Pacific. Although the geographical focus of each is slightly different, they have an internationalist concern in common, and both value a framework of human rights and social and economic development.

Why then are these arguments both from the same perspective? They both argue that gender equality brings social and economic benefits for all, but that a number of challenges remain in its implementation. Neither relies heavily on evidence, choosing instead to depend on a number of general claims. Both assume a link between the specific and the general, that the social and economic empowerment of women will lead to social and economic benefits for all, without considering other variables which may have an impact. These assumptions are also linked to their international context, where social and economic development is seen as inextricably connected to a framework of human rights.

Comparing opposing perspectives

We can use the same set of techniques to pick out differences in these factors, and identify arguments which come from opposing perspectives.

ACTIVITY 3.03

Read the following two arguments. They are both about doping in sport, the use of performance-enhancing drugs by athletes.

- Make a list of the differences between them, and any similarities.
- How would you summarise the differences between their perspectives?

Extract 1: Let's just be honest and allow drugs in sport

As far as I can tell, there are two major objections to unrestrained doping, neither of which actually makes much sense.

The first is about the athletes' welfare: taking banned substances can cause harm. Which is true, but surely those harms could be reduced if those substances were produced legally and properly regulated?

…

The other objection is about fairness. Why should sporting contests be decided according to whichever participant or team has the best chemist? Again, specious. Almost every serious sporting contest on earth is decided at least in part by the participants' resources, their access to the best training, the best nutrition, the best technology and the best support.

…

Brutal? Gladiatorial? Yes, but would it really be that different to what we have today? Professional sport is about physically-exceptional people willingly doing extraordinary things with their bodies in order to entertain the crowds. Allowing doping and the rest would just make sport more entertaining – and more honest.

James Kirkup (2015), 'Let's just be honest and allow drugs in sport', The Telegraph (4 June 2015).

Extract 2: Why it's time to legalise doping in athletics

It is clear that zero-tolerance towards drugs isn't working. It is not stopping people from cheating. It is not providing assurances to the public that good performances are clean. Even the data we have now is likely to underestimate the problem. "Non suspicious" blood data does not prove that no doping technique has been used, only that it did not exceed a certain range, or vary beyond a certain degree.

The career and livelihood of an athlete depends on winning. There are enormous rewards for winners and not much out there for anyone else. And set against that pressure in favour of doping, there is very little chance of getting caught (one estimate is 2% of tested athletes). Psychologists have shown that the lower the risk of being caught, the greater the number of cheats. The greater the number of perceived cheats, the more likely people are to join them.

…

We could increase the testing to a level where the odds of getting caught are higher. It would help, but would not catch everyone. For example, homogenous blood transfusions and other common methods of doping are undetectable at present. Blood passports have been thought to both limit the extent of doping, and to make it easier to dope – by providing a set of limits to work to. Mark Daly, an investigative journalist, describes how he "passed" the biological passport system while using EPO*.

Julian Savulescu (2015), Uehiro Professor of Practical Ethics at the University of Oxford and Louis Matheson Distinguished Visiting Professor, Monash University, The Conversation *(28 August 2015).*

*EPO: a performance-enhancing drug used in sport

Reflection: The most obvious similarity, and perhaps the most surprising, between these two arguments is that they reach the same conclusion. Both argue for the legalisation of performance-enhancing drugs. In Kirkup's case this is for sport in general, and for Savulescu, for athletics in particular. Yet when we look at the other components of their perspectives, they differ markedly.

Conclusion and reasons

As we have seen, both arguments reach the same conclusion. However, their reasoning differs. For Kirkup, doping should be legalised for two reasons. Firstly, the possible physical harm done by performance-enhancing drugs can be more effectively reduced if they are legally produced and regulated. Secondly, doping does not produce an unfair increase in performance because athletes have always used any additional resources they might have to perform better than their rivals. This means that sporting competitions are not about fairness, but entertainment for the spectators.

Savulescu does not argue on the basis of safety or fairness. Instead, his argument for permitting doping is that the methods used to detect and prevent it are ineffective. Because of this, there is no point in using them.

Assumptions

Each argument also differs in its assumptions. Savulescu makes the largest single assumption when he moves from the reasons for the ineffectiveness of doping controls to the conclusion that doping should be legalised. He assumes that this is the only response to the difficulties in enforcing the ban on performance-enhancing drugs. Any other measures, or improvements to the detection system, are discounted. Kirkup also makes some more general assumptions, on which the whole of his argument relies. One of these is also a weakness in reasoning, as he excludes any other reasons one might wish to compete physically with others, such as the satisfaction of developing one's own capabilities through training, or pride in being recognised as the victor in a competition. Instead, athletes are presented as defeating their opponents at all costs, or only being concerned with entertaining their audience.

Evidence

There are more striking differences in how each argument uses evidence. Savulescu provides statistical evidence of the likelihood of being caught, psychological evidence of the effect that would have on behaviour, and medical evidence of how testing methods can be defeated.

In contrast, Kirkup employs very little evidence at all, relying largely on assertion to make his claims about how regulation would reduce harm and allowing drug-based resources would increase entertainment and simply extend what is already happening.

Context

When we come to the context of each argument, the other differences in perspective are confirmed and to a certain extent explained. Kirkup is a journalist, and writes from a journalistic perspective. Savulescu is a university philosopher specialising in the practical applications of ethics, the study of right and wrong. This accounts both for their different lines of reasoning and the more careful use of a variety of evidence by Savulescu, rather than relying on assertion. Although he includes a key assumption within his line of reasoning, he also relies on fewer general assumptions, and these do not compromise the structure of his argument, as they do with Kirkup.

For these reasons, we could conclude that, although their arguments advocate the same thing, Savulescu's perspective in doing so is more convincing, and argumentatively stronger. This does not mean of course that there are not other arguments from a similar perspective to Kirkup's which would strengthen his, but this might be a judgement we reach based on this pair.

Perspectives and active reading

As well as being introduced to perspectives, we have also been developing our active reading skills in this section of the chapter. Our understanding of perspectives, however, has allowed us to move beyond the reading, analysis and evaluation of single arguments, and to deal much more confidently with pairs, using the components of a perspective as dimensions along which we can compare and contrast them.

Part of your development as a Global Perspectives & Research student is the ability not only to identify and evaluate argument, evidence and context in individual sources but also to compare them with other sources you have evaluated. The examples we have explored focus on pairs of arguments, and making a judgement on how their perspectives compare. When you are asked to do this, it will often be through a comparative phrase: to what extent is one document 'stronger' or 'more convincing' than another. When you are doing this you will be identifying the different parts that combine to make their perspectives, and weighing them up again each other to make a decision on which one is stronger, or more convincing, or more successful in challenging the other. There will be an opportunity to practise this yourself at the end of this chapter. In order to write essays, however, or research a topic as a team, you will need to locate and organise larger groups of sources, and this is what we will turn to next.

Deconstruction

Reconstruction

KEY TERM

research: a search for information on a topic

3.02 Locating sources of perspectives

In order to locate sources of your own in order to identify and develop perspectives, you will need to do **research**. The meaning of research is to seek, or search out, information on something, and as a Global Perspectives & Research student it is of crucial importance that you develop as a researcher in order to locate the best possible sources and evidence for the perspective you are evaluating.

Selecting categories of source

The first step in research is to recognise the importance of selecting appropriate materials. We saw in Chapter 2 that it is important to select the strongest possible example of each argument, from the most credible source. This means that you should be aware of the potential types of source from which you are selecting, and focus in on those which are most likely to produce this. A helpful starting point is this list of different kinds of source:

1   Sensationalist media
   - primarily seeks out popularity with its readers
   - uses unverified information which is hard to distinguish from rumour and speculation
   - is heavily biased in its presentation of arguments
   - has very limited expertise and a poor reputation.

2   Popular media
   - commercial interests make popularity with readers a key objective
   - information is generally second-hand, with sources sometimes identified, but this is inconsistent
   - tends to be neutral, except where there is a clear interest in creating entertainment or controversy
   - has limited expertise, but reputation can vary from poor to good.

3   Serious general interest
   - interests tend to be defined by maintaining a good reputation for accuracy and effectiveness, but can also be distorted by a desire to cater for a particular audience (usually associated with particular political views or other beliefs)
   - nearly all information is second-hand, but it is usually corroborated
   - sets out to be neutral, although there may a subtle social or political bias
   - expertise and reputation tend to be good.

4   Scholarly
   - contains peer-reviewed articles, which have been checked by recognised experts in a specific academic field prior to publication
   - has a very high reputation and level of expertise, although conclusions are still based on specific evidence and assumptions and can be challenged
   - there is a high level of neutrality, and arguments tend to be explicit about the position they take
   - the articles contain a variety of types of evidence, and evidence is used to closely support each claim.

Deconstruction

Reconstruction

Given the need to provide the strongest possible sources, it is likely that you will be selecting sources from the third and fourth categories only.

ACTIVITY 3.04

Before you start to look for suitable arguments in each of the categories we have discussed as being appropriate, you will need to know where you can locate them and which publications and other places to look in.

Start by making a list of all the sources you know about, in your country or context, and place them under each of the four categories we have just listed. Use the notes below to help you consider and discuss your choices.

1   These might be specific websites, newspapers or magazines which can be defined as sensationalist. If you are looking for examples here, you can often find them by the cash tills of newsagents. On the internet, sensationalist articles are sometimes known as 'clickbait': links to stories as advertisements in other pages which often have a focus on celebrity news, or something apparently strange or unusual, and designed to tempt you to click and therefore stop reading the article you were previously focused upon.

2   The popular media will be distinct to this, and might well be promoted on television or in print advertisements. Quite often, you will recognise these websites, print publications or television programmes in your own context by the variety of articles they provide. Some will be on more serious political or cultural topics, and will use some evidence and argument to support their claims. Others will have a more obvious commercial or controversial motivation, and will either rely on assertion or will select evidence in such a way as to present a noticeably biased case. Also bear in mind here that the medium of the publication is less important than its neutrality, expertise and use of evidence. In all of the categories, you are likely to find the same publication with a print and online presence (or sometimes a variety of online formats), but this does not alter the nature of the arguments themselves, or your evaluation of them.

broadsheet: newspaper traditionally printed on a larger sheet of newsprint, but now found both in print and online. Usually contains articles of serious general interest.

tabloid: newspaper traditionally printed on a smaller sheet of newsprint, but now found both in print and online. Contains articles which are sensationalist or part of the popular media.

3   You will want to pay most attention to the third category of serious general interest, as this is a range of sources you will aim to select in your work for Global Perspectives & Research, rather than exclude. Start here with a category of newspapers which are sometimes known as '**broadsheets**'. This is a historical definition because they are traditionally printed on a larger size of paper than '**tabloid**' papers (which tend to be in the sensationalist or popular media category). This is not always the case now, and newspapers in this category are as likely to be found online as in print, but it should allow you to identify suitable examples. You should also check here with your school's library, and see which publications, especially magazines, they have chosen subscribe to – although for a general reader, these will have a more professional than popular focus, and be organised around specific professional areas, such as politics, cultural debate, economics or science.

4   At this stage, the final category (scholarly) might be more of an optional or extension task. Scholarly journals and books are usually written by university academics in specific specialised areas. They are peer reviewed, which means that they are checked by other academics who are recognised experts in that field. They have much higher standards of evidence which they must keep to than arguments in the other categories, and can also be much more challenging in the level of reading required to access them. They are usually purchased or subscribed to by universities rather than schools or public libraries, but you may well also find them in these settings. As we saw with Julian Savulescu's argument in favour of doping in sport, sometimes university academics write for serious general interest publications, and use some of the detail and precision of evidence we might more usually expect to find in scholarly sources.

Discussion point

As you gather together lists of publications under each of these categories, you may wish to discuss them with another student, or in class with your teacher, and see if you agree in your findings. You may wish to produce a wall display or other form of collective presentation of your findings.

Focusing on arguments

Remember that in Global Perspectives & Research we are interested in identifying, analysing, evaluating and comparing arguments, in the specific sense we have defined of reasons leading to a conclusion. The Critical Path is organised around making and using arguments. This means that you should ensure that you select arguments in your research, and not other kinds of source.

Reflection: At this point, you might like to look back at Section 2.02 to remind yourself of what arguments are, and how to recognise the differences between arguments and other types of text.

When you are researching, you will be selecting sources with conclusions, which make claims that you are being asked to accept, and are supported by at least some reasons in doing this. You should *not* select:

- explanations: these state something which is known to be true (such as something that has happened, or a scientific fact about the natural world), and then provide reasons which explain it.
- descriptions: these provide statements or evidence about something, but do not draw conclusions from it.
- rhetoric: this uses persuasive language rather than reasons to attempt to convince us of something.
- assertions: these are entirely composed of claims that we are asked to accept, but without any reasons or evidence supporting them.

Searching for the right arguments

Once you have selected the right category of source, and focused on arguments, you will still need to select the right arguments for the topic or issue you are researching. Many students attempt to do this initially perhaps by browsing generally through books, newspapers or magazines in their school library, or more usually by 'searching Google', simply because it is the most used and most easily available search tool for the internet. Both methods of searching are in fact broadly correct, but do have their limitations. A more systematic and thoughtful procedure is more likely to lead to effective results.

Discussion point

Talk as a class about the methods you normally use to look for information. How successful do these tend to be, and what problems have you encountered with them?

The first step is to identify the **key words** for the area you would like to research. A good starting point might be the syllabus description of the topic you are working on. For example, the sources on gender earlier in this chapter are related to the syllabus **topic** of Gender Issues. This will provide an initial focus for your research and might even provide a useful range of sources for you to read initially. Having done this, you will probably find that the range of results you find is very broad, probably unmanageably so. You will need to add more search terms in order to reduce the results, and refine your research to a more manageable area. A good way of doing this is to make use of the **themes** for study described in the Global Perspectives & Research syllabus.

There are seven themes:

- culture
- economics
- ethics
- environment
- politics
- science
- technology.

KEY TERMS

key word: individual word or phrase which can be focused upon in order to refine or clarify understanding of a particular topic or area

topic: in this case, an area for study as defined in the list of topics in the Cambridge International AS & A Level Global Perspectives & Research syllabus

theme: approach to a topic, in this case particularly the seven listed in the Cambridge International AS & A Level Global Perspectives & Research syllabus. The combination of a theme with a topic can help to define a perspective on that topic.

You may think of each of these as potential perspectives on the topic: selective routes for approaching particular parts of it. Each theme has a different emphasis on the types of argument it requires, the evidence it uses, the assumptions it makes and the contexts from which its sources come. We saw in both this chapter and in Chapter 2 that an economic approach to a topic – for example, focusing on the income or profit it generates – will produce potentially quite different conclusions to an ethical one that is concerned with whether it is morally right or wrong according to a specific set of rules or expectations. Equally, as with the topic of sport, and the issue of doping in sport, even when different sources were both arguing for doping to be permitted, the arguments themselves, and hence the perspectives, were quite different depending on whether the thematic approach was scientific (do the tests work?) or ethical (is it fair to use additional resources to enhance performance?).

ACTIVITY 3.05

In order just to see the impact of refining key words, it is very interesting to use a variety of search tools with a single set of key words, starting with 'gender', which we have been discussing.

1   Use Google to search for the word 'gender'. How many results do you get?

2   Now try adding one of the themes (e.g. 'gender ethics' or 'gender technology').

3   Often the word 'argument' or 'debate' can narrow the range of results further, and focus them on arguments which are appropriate for the study of Global Perspectives & Research using the Critical Path.

Now repeat this sequence of steps using the following:

1   Your own school library's electronic catalogue, if it has one. Your school librarian or teacher can tell you how to access it.

2   The public library electronic catalogue for your own local area, if there is one. Here are some examples:

   •   East Sussex Public Libraries: https://e-library.eastsussex.gov.uk

   •   New York Public Library: http://browse.nypl.org/

3   The website scholar.google.com which produces results containing scholarly sources only.

As extended tasks, you could also try:

4   Completing this search using the search facility of a serious general interest magazine. *The Economist* is an example of this and has a search page at http://www.economist.com/search/. Your school may have a subscription to this or other magazines or journals in other thematic areas.

5   Following the steps using a university library catalogue. Examples of these are the University of Sussex in the UK (http://www.sussex.ac.uk/library/) and the University of Sydney in Australia (https://library.sydney.edu.au/).

Reflection: Google's main search engine is the most commonly used and produces the most wide-ranging information. Searching for 'gender' at the time of writing confirms this by producing nearly 3.5 billion results. Yet simply adding 'ethics' reduces this to 73 million. Adding in 'debate' reduces the number further still, to only 18 million, and browsing the first few is likely to produce ideas for further refinement depending on the planned focus.

The other search engines and catalogues produce a smaller range of results which are more focused in different directions. Google Scholar has less than 1 million hits for 'gender ethics debate', but these are all scholarly arguments in peer-reviewed books and journals, and may not be the best starting point. For the public library catalogues, a different set of keywords might be required in order to produce a usable set of results, and these might be for books rather than shorter arguments in newspapers, magazines or journals.

The most focused results are for the search engines of individual publications. *The Economist*, for example, has under 2,000 hits for 'gender ethics debate', and the majority are for shorter, argumentative pieces. Broadsheet newspapers also tend to have their own online search facilities, and these are also well worth employing in order to produce a more precise selection of sources, especially from a specific thematic area or perspective. In many cases the search can be narrowed further still to the editorial section (sometimes called 'op-ed', or opinion-editorial) which is more likely to produce arguments alone.

Reading skills for research

Searching for the right arguments needs to be supported by reading, but these skills are quite different to the active reading which is required for analysing and evaluating, or deconstructing, individual arguments. Instead, you will need to become better at **scanning** and **skimming** texts. These are two types of reading which have different purposes, but are both adapted to rapidly processing, rather than carefully and closely considering, written materials.

Scanning is the first step of considering a list of research results, and excluding irrelevant items while selecting ones which are worthy of further investigation. When you scan, you are searching for a specific word or phrase which is relevant to the aim of your search, and letting your eye run over everything else so that you do not process it at all. For example, having searched for 'sports doping ethics', selecting the topic of international sport, the issue of doping and the thematic approach of ethics, you might scan for the word 'legalisation' in order to pick out possible arguments in favour of permitting it. Alternatively, scanning for 'against' or 'wrong' or 'unethical' is likely to identify arguments against doping.

Another purpose of scanning is to identify the category of the source, ruling out results from publications which are sensationalist or based on popular opinion, as well as personal arguments made by individuals. This makes it much more likely that you will have a list of sources from the category of serious general interest, or ones which are scholarly.

Once you have scanned through your initial set of research results, you will have a smaller list which you can **skim**. This is a technique for processing individual sources in order to make a decision about whether they are relevant and worth actively reading, or deconstructing, in greater detail in order to evaluate and possibly use them in constructing arguments of your own. Skimming involves reading the title of the source as the best summary of the content as well as the first and final paragraphs, which are most likely to contain a conclusion if one is present. It also involves reading any subheadings in the source as well as the first sentence of each paragraph. In a well-written text, these **topic sentences** summarise the content of the paragraph they begin. The subheadings and topic sentences, taken together, allow the overall structure of the argument, if one is present, to become more clearly visible.

The benefit of skimming is to verify the results of the initial scanning stage: does the content of each source match the key words identified in the summary? It also allows each result to be assessed as to whether it actually is an argument, with a conclusion and reasons, and what the broad structure and focus of that argument are.

KEY TERMS

scanning: very quickly searching through a large volume of information for specific key words or phrases

skimming: quickly moving through an individual source in order to pick out clues to its content and purpose

KEY TERM

topic sentence: the first sentence of a paragraph which summarises its content, including the argument it represents

Deconstruction

Reconstruction

ACTIVITY 3.06

1   Choose one of the search tools described in Activity 3.05 (e.g. a search engine like Google, a library catalogue or the search tool of an individual publication).
2   Decide on an issue you would like to research and a thematic focus, and conduct a search using key words based on this.
3   Scan through the results to identify which results you will open in order to read further.
4   Skim these texts and make another, smaller list of relevant, appropriate arguments for active reading in more depth.

Reflection: You should find, as in the example in Activity 3.06, that as you go through each step the number of results becomes smaller and more focused. Using the techniques of scanning and skimming should have enabled you to narrow the scope even further. You can also consider how using these steps might help you in your research for both the essay and team project. These are dealt with in more detail in later chapters.

Note-taking tools for research

Recording what you have found when doing research is as important as the process of identifying and narrowing the range of materials. There are four main stages involved in this:

1   scanning the initial results of your search in order to produce a longer list of possible sources
2   skimming the individual items on the initial long list in order to produce a shortlist for closer consideration
3   taking notes on each item in the shortlist to show the results of your deconstruction of their arguments and evidence.

It is very likely that your search will locate more sources than you list, and that your first list will be longer than your shortlist. In order to find the best, most useful sources, you will discard many more than you eventually use in any work that you produce. The skill of excluding sources, and the decisions not to use most of what you find, are fundamental to producing high-quality research results.

Be prepared to repeat this process multiple times for the same piece of research as well. You will want to experiment with different key words for your issue, use alternative themes as a way of exploring different perspectives and modify your searches in order to capture each side of the debate.

You will also need to consider how you will record all of this. Dealing with many sources, multiple avenues of searching and changes of direction makes it easy to lose track of what you have found, what you understand about it and how you might make use of it. There are a number of methods you might use here.

1   Pen and paper
    •   Advantages: This is the simplest, cheapest and most straightforward method. You could use sheets of file paper stored in a binder or a notebook, and divide your notes into binders or sections.
    •   Disadvantages: As a method, it works less well with sources which are stored in an electronic medium and computer-based search engines, which make up the majority

of research materials now available. Transcribing, or copying over, results from a computer and back again is slow and likely to produce errors.

2 Electronic documents stored on a computer
- Advantages: This avoids many of the limitations of pen and paper. You can copy web addresses and other details from texts straight into the document. As the document is stored electronically, it is less likely to suffer loss and damage, especially if you use a cloud storage service to keep it backed up.
- Disadvantages: It can be hard to locate information unless you are careful how you organise your filing system. Copying and pasting large volumes of information can also make it hard to distinguish your own work from material you have found. This is a potentially significant problem which is discussed in more detail in Chapters 4 and 5.

3 Specialised note-taking software or online service
- Advantages: You might opt for an online service which is especially designed for note taking. Examples are Evernote and OneNote. This has many of the benefits of individual electronic documents, but is designed for storing and retrieving information, so comes with features designed to help you organise your notes and search for specific information amongst a large quantity of data. Services like Evernote and OneNote also store information in the cloud, so your notes are backed up and can be simultaneously accessed on different devices.
- Disadvantages: It can be harder to learn and set up a note-taking service correctly, and some might also have a financial cost attached to them. They also carry the same dangers of copying and pasting information from others directly into your own notes, so it is very important to label carefully what you have found.

ACTIVITY 3.07

Choose one of the three methods above and use it to record your search for suitable sources around a specific issue. Reflect on the advantages and disadvantages you experience yourself, and how you attempted to overcome them.

If you are working with others, you could each try a different method to undertake the same research task, and compare your findings. Which works best for you?

Discussion point

Discuss the three methods listed above with members of your class and share any prior experiences you have had with them, or the experiences you have had while doing Activity 3.07. Which systems have people found to be more or less useful and why?

How to take notes on individual sources

Once you get to the stage of 'taking notes' on individual sources you have found, you need to be very careful to make sure that you know exactly what you mean by this. A good set of notes for some research for Global Perspectives & Research will contain the following:

- Clear information to help you reliably locate where the original source came from. This would include the author, title, publication and date of the source, as well as the URL (web address) if it was online. A library source may also include the library catalogue number.

- Direct quotations from the source using the original words found there. These include quotation marks so that it is clear what comes from the original.

- Paraphrases of material from the source. It might be more appropriate to include short summaries of points from the source in your own words. These do not have quotation marks, but are clearly linked to your notes for that source.

- Direct quotations or paraphrases, which may also include labels to indicate the conclusion of the source's argument, lines of reasoning, evidence, assumptions and notes on the context of the publication or author, including additional information you have found out. Using the framework for deconstruction means your notes are much more likely to be useful in the next stage of your work.

- Your own evaluative judgements and ideas for further development of your research. It is a good idea to use a specific symbol such as an asterisk (*) to indicate these to distinguish your own material from notes on the source.

As an example, here is a short article on renewable energy (from the issue of alternatives to oil) and a set of notes on it using these principles:

Source: How Costa Rica runs on renewable energy – and why it's so hard to replicate

Costa Rica has spent nearly half of 2016 running entirely on renewable energy.

The Central American country has spent 150 days without burning fossil fuels for electricity, including a 76 day straight run between June and September. It has minimised its carbon footprint on a huge scale, putting other countries to shame. But, how has it done it?

Costa Rica has four hydropower stations, which generated 80 per cent of the country's electricity in August. The rest came from solar and wind energy.

So why hasn't the rest of the world followed suit? With a population of nearly 4.9 million and an area of less than 20,000 square miles, Costa Rica doesn't need as much energy as other countries. It also has the perfect conditions – mountainous terrain, rain and access to the shoreline – for hydropower.

However, it is not the only country to leave fossil fuels behind. The EU set renewable energy goals for 2020, but Sweden, Bulgaria and Estonia managed to meet these eight years ahead of schedule. Bonaire, a small Caribbean island, currently produces all its energy from renewable sources.

Aimee Meade (2015), 'How Costa Rica runs on renewable energy – and why it's so hard to replicate', The Independent (15 September 2016).

Notes

'How Costa Rica runs on renewable energy – and why it's so hard to replicate'

Aimee Meade, *The Independent*, 15 September 2016

https://www.indy100.com/article/how-costa-rica-runs-on-renewable-energy-and-why-its-so-hard-to-replicate-7311936

* Independent is UK serious general interest newspaper, now online only.

* Aimee Meade describes herself as a journalist and editor and 'expert in growing engaged, connected communities' (biography on Twitter: @AimeePage)

Costa Rica spent 150 days in 2016 running on renewable energy – more than any other country – including '76 day straight run between June and September'

Energy came from hydropower, solar, wind

* Article starts with evidence about energy use in Costa Rica. Argument at end.

Conclusion: Costa Rica is in an unusual energy situation

Reasons: (1) 'doesn't need as much energy as other countries'

Evidence for (1) population 4.9 million, area 20,000 square miles, 'mountainous terrain, rain and access to the shoreline' adapted to hydropower

* Also some counter-evidence to Costa Rica's uniqueness: worth further investigation into these examples.

Sweden, Bulgaria and Estonia ahead of EU 2020 renewable energy goals

Caribbean island of Bonaire 100% renewable
* how significant is this evidence?

Summary

In this chapter we have:

- explored what a perspective is
- learnt to appreciate the value of holding alternative perspectives
- listed the elements of a perspective in terms of its arguments
- used pairs of sources to draw out the differences and similarities between perspectives
- used an analysis of perspectives to organise and evaluate groups of sources around issues and debates
- listed and evaluated the usefulness of different categories and types of sources
- outlined a variety of methods for searching for information
- evaluated a range of techniques for recording information obtained through research
- described and explained methods for taking notes on research findings.

This chapter has introduced the crucial concept of the perspective, helping us to understand some of our motivation as students of Global Perspectives & Research: being open to different arguments and ways of understanding the world in order to obtain a different or distinctive understanding. By looking at pairs of sources and comparing them we have also been able to complete the range of active reading tasks required by deconstruction.

The second part of the chapter, on research methods and techniques, laid the groundwork for the rest of the book, which is concerned with your own research, using larger groups of sources. To use these, however, you will need to be able to plan and write essays, as well as produce presentations as part of your team project. It is these forms of communication that we will look at in Chapter 4.

Practising deconstruction with reconstruction

This section of the chapter is divided into three: firstly, developing work with pairs of sources, secondly, establishing the comparison and evaluation of perspectives using more than one source and finally, enhancing research skills, which focuses on what was done in the second half of the chapter in light of these comparative skills. Each section is designed to build on the one before. You can either work through each section in turn or choose the section that you feel is at the most appropriate level for you. You should see a progression of difficulty through the three levels, but they are also linked in this chapter to the distinctive skills we have established.

These sections use the topic of **genetic engineering**, one of the topics listed in the Global Perspectives & Research syllabus. However, you should be able to employ the principles of your learning here to a wide variety of other topics in the research you do and examination questions you answer.

Establishing work with pairs of documents

Read the following pair of sources. This is the beginning of an exchange of letters published in *The Independent* between a supporter and an opponent of genetically modified (GM) crops. The first source is a letter from Mark Lynas, an author who supports GM technology. The second is a letter replying to him by Claire Robinson, who works for GMWatch, an organisation campaigning against GM.

Document 1

Dear Claire,

…

I was on your side 15 years ago, opposing GM crops, when there was little evidence of their safety and the precautionary principle seemed apt. But since then sufficient published data has accumulated (now totaling hundreds of peer-reviewed papers) that there is now an overwhelming scientific consensus on the safety of GM technology.

I suspect you might deny this, just as climate change deniers refuse to accept the wisdom of the 1,500 experts who make up the Intergovernmental Panel on Climate Change. So let me quote to you two sentences from statements produced by the board of the American Association for the Advancement of Science, one of the most prestigious scientific societies in the world.

The first reads: "The scientific evidence is clear: global climate change caused by human activities is occurring now, and it is a growing threat to society." The second reads: "The science is quite clear: crop improvement by the modern molecular techniques of biotechnology is safe." I admit, it was this contradiction between promoting climate change science and denying GM science that made me change my mind on the latter issue. I wonder: now that the experts have spoken, what would it take to change yours?

Best wishes,

Mark

Document 2

> Dear Mark,
>
> I agree it's vital to make judgements about the safety of GM crops based on empirical evidence.
>
> …
>
> Many scientific organisations have issued statements that cast doubt on GMO safety and/or say that the jury is still out. Even the statement by the American Association for the Advancement of Science board of directors that you cite was condemned by 21 dissenting scientists, including members of the AAAS, as "an Orwellian argument". The scientists warned that the herbicides with which GMOs are grown "may induce detrimental health effects even at low exposure levels".
>
> That warning has now gained the support of the IARC, the cancer research arm of the World Health Organisation, which has declared that glyphosate herbicide, used on over 80% of all GM crops, probably causes cancer. It's also largely responsible for a massive 90% decline of the monarch butterfly.
>
> …
>
> Yours,
>
> Claire

Remember that in order to compare the perspectives of these two documents, we need to compare these features of each:

- reasons
- conclusions
- assumptions
- evidence
- context.

1 Read again what you are told about the context of each author. What are the similarities and differences between their backgrounds and positions? What might this lead you to expect about their arguments?

   As an extension task, you might do some research work into each to find out what they did before and afterwards.

2 How does the evidence used by each writer compare? Do they rely on the same type of evidence, and what does this show about them?

3 What does each author conclude, and how does this differ?

4 What does Mark Lynas assume about Claire Robinson when he says 'I suspect you might deny this, just as climate change deniers refuse to accept the wisdom of the 1,500 experts who make up the Intergovernmental Panel on Climate Change'?

5 To what extent is Claire Robinson's argument more or less convincing than that of Mark Lynas? Are there any assumptions you are making here which might lead you to that conclusion?

Developing work with pairs of sources
Read the following pair of documents, which are also on the topic of GM crops.

Document 1

Fear about GM crops is not backed up by facts

GM foods are widely misunderstood by the public, but offer advantages that we forgo at our peril.

William Reville is a former professor of biochemistry at University College Cork in the Republic of Ireland.

…

A genetically modified organism is one whose DNA has been altered artificially by "genetic engineering" in order to confer a new desirable characteristic on the organism. Nearly all corn and soybeans grown in the US are genetically modified. Genetic engineering can transfer selected genes from one organism to another. For example, plants can be protected against insect pests by incorporating a gene for anti-pest toxin from a bacterium into the plant. This toxin, used in conventional agriculture, is safe for human consumption.

Of course, all food derived from plants is genetically modified, because farmers have been improving food plants for thousands of years by repeatedly crossing them with relatives having more desirable characteristics. It takes many years to produce a commercially viable crop this way, so plant breeders introduced new genetic manipulation tools to supplement conventional breeding well before the advent of GM foods, for example blasting plants with radiation or chemicals to cause genetic mutations and then picking promising new mutations.

In contrast to slow, imprecise traditional breeding methods, precise plant improvements can be achieved in one generation with genetic engineering. In this case a single gene, or small group of genes, is introduced into the plant, imparting specific desirable characteristics such as tolerance of salt, drought or frost, or resistance to disease.

…

Comprehensive studies have consistently attested to the safety of genetic engineering technology. As long ago as 1987 the US National Academy of Sciences concluded that plants produced by genetic engineering techniques pose no new or different risks to human health or the environment than those produced using other breeding methods. Since then, the EU and a number of countries have reached the same conclusion.

GM crops offer many advantages that we forgo at our peril. For example, Asian governments have yet to approve insect-resistant higher-yield genetically modified rice (Golden Rice), engineered to deliver vitamin A (rice normally has no vitamin A), despite the fact that vitamin A deficiency kills more than a million people annually and irreversibly blinds half a million people.

The world's population continues to balloon, and by 2050 the world will have to grow 70 per cent more food to keep up with that growth. The widespread adoption of genetic engineering technology will be essential to help achieve this goal.

Document 2

Approach GM foods with caution, not total rejection

This article was published in *The Observer*, a Ugandan newspaper. The author, who is not named in the article, lectures in bioethics at Uganda Martyrs University.

. . .

Herbicides resolve the problem of weeds but may be hazardous to human health, animals and the environment. A report released on March 20, 2015, by a panel of scientists from the World Health Organization's International Agency for Research on Cancer (IARC) deemed glyphosate to be 'probably carcinogenic (cancer-causing) material to humans.' Glyphosate is the active ingredient in the most commonly used herbicide, Roundup.

The claim by the IARC is, however, disputed by Monsato, the multinational agrochemicals and agricultural biotechnology company that manufactures Roundup. What is clear, however, is that carcinogenic agents or materials may cause cell cycle dysregulation to occur or inhibit DNA synthesis, which may result in cancer.

. . .

Environmentalists are also concerned about ecological disruption. Unwanted supper weeds may emerge when the indigenous weeds develop resistance to herbicides. Another concern is the alteration and elimination of natural species. The seed head of the GMO plants does not self-propagate like the natural indigenous seed.

The implication is that every planting season, the farmers will have to depend on foreign manufacturers with patents, and on local agents who rely on market forces to determine prices.

Given also that genetics is at its infancy in Uganda, the agricultural sector will have to depend on foreign scientists to generate GM seeds, herbicides, and pesticides. The small farmer with limited capital will most likely abandon farming.

But the most immediate impact of GMO introduction in Uganda will be more felt in the agricultural export sector. While Uganda can ably compete with big economies in organic agricultural produce, it is likely that the introduction of GM crops will diminish trade opportunities. Why should developed countries buy GM food from Uganda when they can produce it in quantities in their own countries?

However, this said, genetic engineering in agriculture is work in progress. We can approach it with caution, but it is unwise to reject it wholly.

1 Compare the perspectives represented by these two documents. What are their similarities and differences?

2 To what extent is the argument in Document 2 stronger than that in Document 1?

Enhancing research skills

Using the skills you have gained from Section 3.02, locating sources of perspectives, find further sources yourself on the issue of genetically modified foods.

You can either:

- find two more sources which would support the perspective shown by Mark Lynas and two more sources which would support the perspective shown by Claire Robinson in the Establishing work with pairs of documents section above

Or you can:

- find several more sources which would support each of the two perspectives you identified in the Developing work with pairs of documents section above.

Whichever task you choose, please ensure that:

- the sources you find are arguments
- they come from publications in at least the 'serious general interest' category
- you make use of at least some of the search tools described in this chapter to find them
- once you have located your chosen articles, you make notes on them as described in this chapter.

You should be able to use your notes to confirm that the sources you have found match the perspectives you are looking for and meet the other criteria.

Chapter 4
Deconstruction, reconstruction and reflection: planning the essay

Learning aims

By the end of this chapter, you should be able to:

- understand the role of reflection in essay writing
- define what an essay is and consider its importance
- use topics and themes to select suitable issues for writing essays
- link issues to different perspectives in essays
- analyse and evaluate effective essay questions
- clarify terms used in questions in order to focus your thinking and arguments.

This chapter will support you with the essay, which is also covered in Chapter 5.

Deconstruction	→	Reconstruction	→	Reflection

Communication and Collaboration

Deconstruction

Reconstruction

Reflection

Introduction

In Chapters 2 and 3 you developed several important sets of skills that build on each other:

- **deconstruction**: the analysis and evaluation of arguments and evidence in individual sources
- **reconstruction**: the organisation of sources into perspectives, and the act of locating groups of sources from specific perspectives

Adding reconstruction to deconstruction also allowed us to compare sources with each other, identifying their conclusions, reasons, evidence and assumptions in order to decide which sources – and perspectives – are more convincing. This was not a matter of deciding which sources were better argued, more credible, or more reliable in their evidence. We saw that it is important to select the strongest possible representative of each perspective when we undertake research to find sources. Instead, it was a matter of becoming conscious of the assumptions made, the evidence used and the conclusions reached by groups of sources in order to decide whether we personally can accept those more than the alternatives we have found.

KEY TERM

reflection: the process of consciously considering what we have read or experienced and the ability to explain the effect it has had on the way we think, feel or act

If we find that we share the assumptions contained within a specific perspective, and we feel that the type of evidence it uses is more convincing than that used by other perspectives, then it is more likely that we will find we share it, and will be able to explain why we share it. This type of thinking, consciously considering the choices we have made, is called **reflection** and is a very important stage in the Critical Path. We will be using it in this chapter to help us plan essays, but as we will also see, reflection has an important role in participating in team projects, as well as in planning and writing research reports. As we explore each of these aspects, we will develop our definition of the term further.

4.01 Why essays?

The noun 'essay' comes from the French verb *essayer*, 'to try' or 'to try out'. This in turn comes from the Latin word *exagium*, which refers to weighing something, considering how heavy it is. Both of these ancestors to the modern English term 'essay' tell us something about its nature, as an essentially experimental or reflective form of writing.

The beginning of its definition in the *Cambridge English Dictionary* is 'a short piece of writing on a particular subject'. When we write essays, we are trying out ideas in order to see what we think about them. They provide a format for considering or thinking through different arguments so that we can reach our own conclusions. It is this flexibility which makes the essay both powerful and challenging as a form of writing.

ACTIVITY 4.01

Reading this book, and following the Global Perspectives & Research course, is probably not the first time you have encountered essay writing in your education.

Make a list of subjects where you have had to write essays, and also note down any examples of specific essay tasks you can remember. If you can, share these with two or three other members of your class and compile a collective list.

- What similarities do you notice between the essays you have previously been set?
- Have there been any significant differences between tasks and subjects?
- What ideas do you have that might explain these differences and similarities?

Reflection: Activity 4.01 has probably shown you that a form as flexible as the essay in general means that our expectations for specific types of essay are likely to be related to their context: what they are being written for, and the purpose they are trying to achieve. This will have consequences for the way the essay is structured, its language and the type of evidence that it uses. For example, the sources of evidence that are acceptable in a history essay are likely to be different to those that can be used in an essay on English literature, because the first is exploring ideas about the understanding of historical events, and the second is rehearsing interpretations of novels, plays or poems. There may, however, be overlaps, for example when an essay chooses to write about the historical circumstances in which a novel was written. Similarly, the structure of argument suitable for attempting to resolve a problem in philosophy is different to the ways in which an essay summarising a geographical investigation might be organised. Often, essays written in school are produced in response to the requirements of particular examination syllabuses, and these might have more specific expectations about the content of the essay which should be produced.

Essays and Global Perspectives & Research

Successful essays written as part of the Global Perspectives & Research course are likely to reflect the expectations of the Critical Path and will be good examples of the academic skills it develops. This means that:

- they will be arguments (conclusions based on reasons), not pieces of rhetorical persuasion, explanations of things already known or descriptions of how things are
- they will use evidence to support their reasons
- evidence will come from a range of different sources, which themselves are arguments, not other kinds of writing
- the essay will be focused on a specific issue, and that issue will be based on the topics listed in the Cambridge International AS & A Level Global Perspectives & Research syllabus
- because it is based on a Global Perspectives & Research topic, it will have global relevance, rather than being meaningful only within a particular local situation
- Global Perspectives & Research essays will be organised around debates between opposing points of view, rather than acknowledging only one approach to the issue

Deconstruction

Reconstruction

Reflection

- the essay will therefore respond to a question which is focused on a global debate around a specific issue
- the essay will understand points of view or approaches as perspectives, and break these down using the different components of a perspective: conclusions, reasons, evidence, assumptions and the context of the source
- as the essay proceeds, it will move between deconstruction and reconstruction, reading and evaluating individual sources, and organising those sources into larger perspectives by weighing up similarities and differences
- essays written for Global Perspectives & Research will always be reflective, consciously considering the similarities and differences between perspectives and weighing them up at the end in order to reach a conclusion.

4.02 Choosing and building essays for Global Perspectives & Research

Before writing an essay, you will need to choose what to write it about, and how to organise that into a shape suitable for an essay. To do that requires some consideration of the relationship between topics, issues, themes and perspectives.

Topics and issues

The Cambridge International AS & A Level Global Perspectives & Research syllabus lists 30 topics for study, of which it is expected that you should cover at least three during your time following the course. As we have already seen, studying more rather than fewer topics is a good thing, because they provide different opportunities to develop the skills of the Critical Path in which we are really interested. They have been chosen because they are relevant to the world today and provide opportunities to organise issues, themes and perspectives around them.

An **issue**, on the other hand, is a specific situation suitable for further study which arises from one of the topics. Although the topics are helpful as starting points, they are too broad to be manageable for an essay or other piece of work. Issues allow us to do this.

For example, if we were to take just one of the topics, that of sustainable futures, these are just some of the possible issues we might consider:

- the use of nuclear energy as an alternative to fossil fuels
- the advantages and disadvantages of wind energy
- whether one source of renewable energy is better than another
- the advantages and drawbacks of recycling
- whether we need economic or political changes to make sustainable living more possible
- whether sustainable living is necessary
- different definitions of 'sustainable' and whether they matter.

As you will see from this list, one topic can easily produce a large number of issues. These can be specific aspects of the topic (for example, a type of energy source, or a sustainable activity, like recycling) or questions that arise from the topic (such as what actions might or might not be necessary, or different ways in which we might approach it or understand it).

The best way to move from the topics to issues is to think about what you know about the topic, what you understand by it, questions you would like to ask and aspects you would like to investigate further. This listing process will help you to clarify your thoughts and open up an agenda for further investigation by focusing on one or more of the topics in further detail.

> **KEY TERM**
>
> **issue:** a specific, more narrowly defined area within a topic which is more suitable for an essay or other piece of work

ACTIVITY 4.02

1   Choose one of the 30 topics listed in the syllabus. Mind-map, either individually or with another student, as many different issues arising from this topic as you can identify.

Reflection point: Look at the issues you have identified in Activity 4.02. Consider or discuss them with other students. What are the different ways in which they break the topic down, or explore different aspects of it? What useful questions do they open up for you? How would you like to explore them further?

It is likely that this exercise will produce a number of different, or even apparently conflicting, issues, but also that they are much more focused and manageable, and could be turned into questions for further research.

Issues and themes

Once we have identified a suitable issue we would like to investigate further, we can use a number of different **themes** to make this easier. Themes are ways of approaching an issue, or highlighting particular aspects of it, and are closely linked to perspectives. Individual issues can be approached in different ways depending on the theme selected, and alternative themes can highlight different areas of evidence or conclusions.

As you saw in Chapter 3, the Cambridge International AS & A Level Global Perspectives & Research syllabus lists seven different themes:

- culture
- economics
- environment
- ethics
- politics
- science
- technology.

KEY TERM

theme: in this case, one of the seven themes listed in the Cambridge International AS & A Level Global Perspectives & Research syllabus, which can be used as an approach to an issue

It is important to remember that the Global Perspectives & Research approach is about skills rather than knowledge, or rather that knowledge comes through the skills and methods we apply. This means that there isn't a defined list of facts, or other kinds of knowledge you need to learn and understand about each theme. Instead, they are invitations to ask different sorts of questions about the issue you are investigating. Here are some of the sorts of questions you could ask:

- **Culture**: Does this issue have implications for how people live together in societies, for the everyday things we do in families, with friends, and in communities, with how we live, work and are entertained?
- **Economics**: Does this issue have implications for trading relationships, or how we buy and sell things and their cost, with money, and the transfer of wealth from one person, or group of people, to another?
- **Environment**: What does this issue mean for the natural world around us, for animals, plants and everything which has not been constructed by human beings, and does it carry implications for how human beings interact with the rest of the world?
- **Ethics**: Does this issue raise questions about what is right and wrong, good and bad – however we define this – with what we should do rather than what we can do?
- **Politics**: What would politicians have to say about this issue, or more broadly, is this an issue governments would need to think about, and would different governments make different decisions about it?

- **Science**: Can this issue be approached scientifically, and is there scientific evidence or methods we can use to improve our knowledge of it or to understand it differently?
- **Technology**: have particular items of technology (types of computing device, communication systems like the internet, ways of displaying, measuring or manipulating information) had an impact on how this issue is understood, or are there current, new or emerging technologies that might make us think about it differently?

These questions are only the start of how we could think about each of the themes, and they can seem overwhelming to begin with. However, focusing them on individual issues can help us begin to make more sense of them.

Take the topic of international law, for example. This is concerned with the use of the law to govern relationships between countries, rather than just what happens within individual countries. Like the other Global Perspectives & Research topics, this can give rise to a number of different issues. One issue, however, is the use of extradition treaties between countries. These are legal agreements which mean that if someone is accused of a crime in another country, then they can be made to return to that country to be put on trial there and face whatever penalty that country sets out for the crime if they are found guilty.

We can ask different questions about this issue depending on the theme we use to approach it:

- **Politics**: Is it a problem if the countries involved have different political systems and different systems of justice which might define, punish and investigate crimes in contrasting ways? Is it important for a good political relationship between countries that extradition be allowed?
- **Ethics**: Is it right to send someone, potentially against their will, to face justice in another country when the case is not yet proven? Would it be right to allow someone to avoid being accountable for their actions by not sending them?
- **Economics**: Do the costs of running a system of extradition outweigh the benefits, especially if those large amounts of money are spent on lawyers and other court costs? Would the political damage to relationships between countries caused by not allowing extradition also carry economic costs in terms of trade between them?

These are not the only themes which could be relevant to this issue. You may think of questions for others, or want to put them in a different order of importance.

ACTIVITY 4.03

Look back to at least one of the issues you identified in Activity 4.02.
- Which of the themes are most relevant to the issue?
- What questions does each of these themes allow you to ask about the issue?
- How do the different themes allow you to think about the issue in alternative ways?

Themes and perspectives

Once you have considered possible themes which might be relevant to the issue, then you can begin to link them to alternative perspectives. As we established in Chapter 3, perspectives are made up of the following components:

- reasons
- conclusions

- assumptions
- evidence
- context.

When we consider an issue according to a theme, we are also making a number of choices about the lines of argument we use, the type of evidence used, the assumptions made and the context of those arguing for it – who they are and where they come from. For example, an ethical argument may make assumptions about acceptable and unacceptable solutions to the problem which an economic argument would not. On the other hand, an economic argument is likely to use evidence of the volumes of goods bought and sold and their costs, which may not be utilised by other themes.

Linking themes to perspectives also allows you to focus on the research needed in order to find sources. Remaining with the issue of extradition, you might ask yourself:

- What political arguments can you find for or against extradition?
- What ethical arguments can you find for or against extradition?
- What economic arguments can you find for or against extradition?

ACTIVITY 4.04

Use the research techniques outlined in Chapter 3 to create a longlist and a shortlist of suitable arguments (from sources which are at least of serious general interest) on the issue of extradition.

Your sources should be organised by theme into different perspectives. As a starting point, create three groups which are political, ethical and economic.

These three groups may include arguments for or against extradition, or both. You may also find that you locate more than one source, from different perspectives on the same extradition case. Examples of these from recent years include Augusto Pinochet, Gary McKinnon and Julian Assange. Focusing your debate on specific cases like this may help you to explore the different themes and perspectives in more detail.

Reflection: Completing this activity fully will probably be challenging and take some time. You will need to use suitable research techniques from Chapter 3 to locate relevant and credible sources, utilising search engines and catalogues to generate a longlist of possible results, and then narrowing this down to a shortlist.

The next step, locating arguments for and against extradition, perhaps in relation to specific cases, should be easier. However, it will require some careful evaluation of the sources you find in order to place them into perspectives.

Take, for example, this pair of sources on the case of Julian Assange, the founder of the political organisation Wikileaks, who took refuge in the Ecuadorean Embassy in London to avoid extradition to Sweden to face charges of rape and sexual assault.

1 'The Guardian view on Julian Assange: no victim of arbitrary detention', *The Guardian*, 4 February 2016, https://www.theguardian.com/commentisfree/2016/feb/04/the-guardian-view-on-julian-assange-no-victim-of-arbitrary-detention

2 Katrin Axelsson and Lisa Longstaff, 'We are Women Against Rape but we do not want Julian Assange extradited', *The Guardian*, 23 August 2012, https://www.theguardian.com/commentisfree/2012/aug/23/women-against-rape-julian-assange

Deconstruction

Reconstruction

Reflection

Deconstruction

Reconstruction

Reflection

Source 1, an editorial by *The Guardian*, a UK newspaper, is in favour of his extradition from an ethical perspective, arguing that it is morally wrong that he should avoid facing a court for the crimes of which he was accused. Source 2, also published in *The Guardian*, but by representatives of an anti-rape pressure group, opposes his extradition from a political perspective, arguing with the assumption that the moves to extradite Assange are motivated by a political desire to suppress the activities of Wikileaks in releasing confidential information, rather than an ethical concern with the crime of rape.

Locating then evaluating sources on this issue in the same way will help you in developing the kind of considerations you need to have in doing research for the essay.

Working independently

A very important part of your development as a Global Perspectives & Research student is having the confidence to identify topics you are interested in from the list available, to discover issues from these that are relevant to you, your fellow students and others in your local community, and to explore thematic approaches and different perspectives which reflect your interests and those of others who might think differently to you.

The ideas in this section are not intended to give you specific topics or issues to write your essay about. Instead, they provide a method for allowing you to build your own. You may do this with the help of your teacher, or with other students you are working with, as well as on your own, but in each case there is a process to follow:

1   Select a topic: Where is my starting point?

2   Identify an issue: What examples of this topic can we notice around us? What problems does this topic show we might have to deal with? What conflicts or debates are associated with it?

3   Consider themes: Do any of the themes suggest particular approaches to the issue? What debates or conflicts do they reveal?

4   Build perspectives: How do these thematic debates match up with specific lines of argument, kinds of evidence, assumptions, authors and publications in sources you find?

This final stage then leads to questions such as which sources and perspectives are most convincing, or which offer the strongest solution to the problems identified by the issue you are considering.

The most important point here is that questions, not answers, are central to what we should be doing. Being inquisitive about the world around us is one of the key qualities you should be developing, and that means being able to ask good questions so you can find answers and solutions of your own. Being able to formulate your own questions on topics, issues, themes and perspectives you have developed yourself is essential to writing essays, and the next section has some ideas and advice to help you to do this.

4.03 Effective essay questions

In Section 4.01, we saw that essays are flexible, experimental, investigative forms of writing, and that Global Perspectives & Research essays reflect this, although they also have several other features linked to the skills being developed by the Critical Path. In Section 4.02 we also saw that deciding what to write about is based on a process which involves opening up questions about topics, issues, themes and perspectives, and is followed independently every time you produce something.

Essays come from questions, and producing an effective question is central to writing a successful essay. This section discusses what good essay questions look like, and gives advice on how to produce good questions of your own.

Types of question

Because you will be producing your own question when you write essays, rather than responding to one that has been written by a teacher or examiner, you need to know more about how questions work than would otherwise be the case.

There are three main kinds of question that appear in essays and also in examinations. Only one of them, however, is actually a question:

- Commands (sometimes called **imperatives**) ask you to do something. An example of this might be 'Explain why women should have equal opportunities for employment' or 'Evaluate whether electric cars are an efficient method of transportation'.

- Statements (sometimes called **declaratives**) describe a situation and imply – suggest without explicitly stating – that this should be analysed and evaluated. Examples here would include 'The ethics of stem cell research' or 'The rise of cultural nationalism'.

- Questions which really are questions (sometimes called **interrogatives**) pose a question using a question mark – for example, 'Should religious organisations be involved in education?' or 'Is the removal of barriers to international trade a good thing?'.

This third alternative, questions which really are questions, or interrogatives, offers a number of advantages for the kind of essays you should be writing for Global Perspectives & Research. The first is that a question requires an answer, so the essay will have to have a conclusion. However, the fact that the question has to be asked at all means that there are different ways of answering it and alternative conclusions. This means that any answer will also be an argument: reasons supporting the selection of one particular conclusion rather than other conclusions. Questions are also useful here because they open up the possibility of alternative points of view or perspectives, rather than directing us towards only one.

By contrast, commands tend to direct the answer in one direction, to do the thing they instruct. This is because the command, often called a **command word**, is followed by a

KEY TERMS

imperative: a question which is phrased as a command, asking the reader to do something specific

declarative: a question which is phrased as a statement, outlining a situation to be described or explored

interrogative: a question framed directly as a question, requiring an answer where a number of alternative answers usually exist. The answer given is usually phrased as a conclusion, supported by reasons and evidence.

command word: in an imperative, the words which contain the command or commands to which the reader should respond. Examples might include 'show' or 'evaluate'.

statement which describes what you have been commanded to do. We can see this in the two examples listed above:

- '*Explain* why' (command word) 'women should have equal opportunities for employment' (statement)
- '*Evaluate* whether' (command word) 'electric cars are an efficient method of transportation' (statement)

In each case, we are working from a statement which could be a conclusion in itself, and this limits the range of our own possible conclusions. The command word directs us to operate in a specific way upon that statement, which again limits the possible range of our deconstruction and reconstruction of different perspectives. Often, this is useful, especially in an examination situation. This includes, as we have seen in Section 2.03 and 3.01, the specific deconstruction tasks tested in written examinations, where you may be asked to *identify* reasons or evidence, for example, or to *evaluate* the strengths and weaknesses of an argument in one or both of the documents as a specific task. However, responding to command words in this way is inappropriately restrictive for the research-based, experimental exploration of an essay.

Statements, on the other hand, can send the essay in no specific direction at all and lead to a response which just describes the situation without arguing for or against a claim. This is too broad for a focused essay, and can also make it difficult to argue evaluatively in a particular direction towards a conclusion. So, 'the ethics of stem cell research' prompts a discussion of the ethics (the moral rights and wrongs) of using stem cells (undifferentiated cells, most often harvested from embryos) for research into medical conditions or other aspects of the human body. While it is true that this discussion might give rise to evaluation of an argument ('Should we use stem cells for research?'), as the statement stands this is not necessary and might even remain at the level of describing what stem cells are, what research into them involves and what the ethical arguments are, without moving on to any other aspects of the Critical Path. (Statements can be useful for some of the tasks you will have to perform as a Global Perspectives & Research student – for example, describing a problem you and your team will tackle in the team project – but we will come to this later in this book.)

Discussion point

Discuss with others where you have previously come across these different types of question, especially in assessed tasks you have had to do, and the different purposes they serve.

ACTIVITY 4.05

Look at the list of example questions we have just discussed:

- **a** Explain why women should have equal opportunities for employment.
- **b** Evaluate whether electric cars are an efficient method of transportation.
- **c** The ethics of stem cell research
- **d** The rise of cultural nationalism
- **e** Should religious organisations be involved in education?
- **f** Is the removal of barriers to international trade a good thing?

For a–d, rewrite each as an interrogative.

For e–f, rewrite each as a declarative and an imperative, choosing your own command words.

Reflection: Reflect on how these rewritings change your understanding of the question, and its suitability for a Global Perspectives & Research essay. You may consider, for example, that the imperatives are effective in pushing you towards one argument on the issue, but reduce the scope for exploring alternatives. The declaratives, on the other hand, on their own, make focus harder. For the interrogatives, it would also be useful to list the alternative arguments they point towards.

Focusing on the issue and setting up a debate

Once we have focused on an interrogative, a good essay question focuses on an issue and clearly organises a debate. Here is an example:

- Can the genetic modification of food provide a solution to global poverty?

This question starts with the overall topic of genetic engineering, and within this focuses on the issue of the genetic modification of food. The debate is about whether this is a solution to global poverty. There is the possibility of finding and reconstructing more than alternative perspectives which either see it as a solution to global poverty or argue that it is not.

For every question you create, you always need to be able to say what the issue is and identify a debate: more than one point of view which conflict with one another, so that you can develop them into perspectives and reach a conclusion which chooses between them.

ACTIVITY 4.06

Consider the following two questions, which are both effective essay titles:
- Should performance-enhancing drugs be allowed in competitive sport?
- Is sustainability possible in developing countries?

For each of these, identify the Global Perspectives & Research topic, the specific issue that is being focused upon, and the debate, including what the alternative perspectives might be.

Reflection: Here is a suggestion about how you might have answered the first of these two questions:

Question: Should performance-enhancing drugs be allowed in competitive sport?

Topic: International Sport

Issue: The use of performance-enhancing drugs by athletes

Debate:

- yes they should be used (e.g. economic perspective that it would increase revenue for sport by reducing need to test and increasing spectacle)
- no (e.g. ethical perspective that no participant in a sporting competition should have an unfair advantage)

What other arguments and perspectives can you identify? What about the second question?

Avoiding some pitfalls in question setting

Just as there are some key things you can focus on in question setting, there are also some things to avoid.

Avoid asking more than one question.

The first is trying to ask two or more questions. Look at this essay title as an example:

- Is the genetic modification of food crops an efficient solution to poverty in developing countries and should we be doing it?

The word *and* gives away the fact that this is actually two questions:

- Is the genetic modification of food crops an efficient solution to poverty in developing countries?
- Should we be genetically modifying food crops?

Both of these questions are potentially effective essay titles. However, each sets up different debate and thematic focus within the same issue.

The first question might be seen to contrast scientific with economic approaches, depending on whether we see the word *efficiency* as the technical feasibility of genetic modification in those contexts (would the biological processes involved operate correctly and reliably?) or as the monetary costs involved (would it cost too much for the communities involved, or not be profitable enough for the companies producing the seeds?).

The second question, on the other hand, signals with the verb *should* that the ethical theme takes the lead. Questions about what we should or should not do can only be answered by reference to an ethical standard of what is considered to be right or wrong. An alternative ethical approach here might be one which claims it is wrong to change the natural functioning of organisms by artificial means. This might be opposed by one which argues that it is wrong to allow people in some parts of the world to go hungry by not using genetic modification to improve yields. Other ethical perspectives might be informed by environmental or political themes, in other words about what the impact of genetic modification of crops would be on the natural environment or on political relationships between governments in different parts of the world.

Consider the scope of the question

Another potential pitfall involves the scope of the question. This might be too narrow, especially if you limit your question to one country or region. Compare these two questions, for example:

- Should immigration be regulated through physical barriers?
- Should a border wall be constructed between the United States and Mexico?

The first question takes the topic of migration and work, and focuses on the issue of the regulation of immigration, setting up a debate between physical barriers and other methods of regulating, or controlling, immigration. The second has selected the same topic, issue and debate, but by specifying a proposed border wall between the United States and Mexico has limited its scope to only the relationship between those two countries. The first question is potentially global, then, but the second is not.

ACTIVITY 4.07

Consider the following question, whose scope is limited to one country:

- Is France right to ban people from covering their faces in public?

This question relates to a law passed in France in 2010, which prohibits the concealing of the face in public areas. Although applying in general to all face coverings, it has most often been associated with a ban on the niquab and burkha, items of clothing worn by Muslim women which conceal the face.

Can you rewrite this question so that it has a global scope, rather than only focusing on one country?

Keep it focused

The final pitfall involves questions which are too broad. The question 'Does God exist?', for example, identifies the existence of God as an issue from the topic of the secular–religious divide, and is certainly able to focus on a debate. However, this is not a successful strategy for a Global Perspectives & Research essay, as that debate is too broad to be dealt with within the word count available and the time you will have while you are following this course and the other studies you are doing. It also does not fit easily within the alternative areas of thematic focus (ethics is perhaps the closest match).

Overly broad questions also tend to be phrased in a way that makes argument and debate using the Critical Path harder to achieve. Look at these two questions, for example:

- What should the role of women be in a globalised world?
- How has the internet affected global political relationships?

Each question does identify a specific topic and locates an issue within it. However, in each case, this issue is too broad to handle well within the available time and space, and the issue is not made easier by the use of the words 'what' and 'how' to begin the question. The words we use to begin questions are called **question stems** and have an important role in determining the type of answer which results. *What* and *how* tend to require a description or explanation in the answer, whereas *is*, *should* or *can*, for example, are more likely to request a conclusion supported by reasons and evidence, and for the essay to decide between alternative approaches or perspectives.

> **KEY TERM**
>
> **question stem:** a word starting a question, such as *what*, *how*, *is*, *should* or *can*, which controls the type of question which is asked and the range of possible responses

4.04 Writing questions and clarifying terms

As Section 4.03 has demonstrated, constructing an appropriate essay question is crucial to producing a successful final outcome. As with the other elements of the Critical Path, it is therefore more important to have a method for developing work of your own, rather than making decisions about tasks and texts which have been prepared for you in advance.

Once you have ensured that your question is an interrogative, not an imperative or declarative, that it engages with an issue and a debate, and that you have only written one question with an appropriate scope, you will need to ensure that it is precise and as focused as possible on the arguments you wish to explore and make yourself. You can do this by clarifying the terms you have used. This means you are ensuring that you have restricted their range of possible meanings as far as is possible so that they mean exactly what you want them to mean, and the content of your essay precisely reflects the focus and parameters of your question.

Deconstruction

Reconstruction

Reflection

Vagueness and ambiguity

The first task is to be able to identify which words in your question are not as precisely focused as they could be. There are two ways in which words can lack precision: **vagueness** and **ambiguity**.

Vague words have a continuous range of meanings where it is not possible to identify individual definitions. The adjective 'efficient', which we have already used several times in example essay questions, is an example of a vague term. It could, for instance, be applied to most of the themes: something is economically efficient if it generates the maximum possible profit for the least amount of expenditure, but a computer is technologically efficient if it produces a high number of computations relative to the time and energy the device consumes. In the environmental domain, efficiency is the minimisation of environmental impact. Overall, efficiency measures the difference between inputs and outputs within a system, but there is a potentially infinite range of types of systems and individual examples to which we could apply that. This means some additional qualification needs to be applied to any use of the term 'efficient' in order to place it more precisely within that range and reduce the possible vagueness.

A word is ambiguous, on the other hand, if there are several different specific meanings it could have but we are not sure which one to select. For example, the word 'global' itself could refer to things related to the planet Earth (if 'globe' means 'planet'), to issues affecting everyone in the world ('the global population'), to every country in the world ('global' rather than national or regional) or even to things of universal relevance ('global' as meaning 'everything'). These four meanings are discrete, or distinctive and individual, and can be specifically defined in themselves, but they all relate to the same word. In order to make clear which one we want to mean, we would either need to use a different word, or define 'global' in such a way as to restrict the possibilities to which it refers.

The best way to see the identification of vagueness and ambiguity in action is to apply it to a question. We can do that with this first draft of a possible Global Perspectives & Research essay question, taken from the topic of artificial intelligence:

- Is artificial intelligence beneficial for humans?

This question meets the criteria for an appropriate Global Perspectives & Research question in the following ways:

1 It is an interrogative, not a declarative or imperative.

2 It is one question, not two or three.

3 It does not specify a single country or region, but could be globally applicable.

4 It uses a question stem, 'is', which produces a debate between more than one alternative, rather than a descriptive one such as 'how' or 'what'.

5 It includes three areas of focus, 'artificial intelligence', 'beneficial' and 'humans', which limits the scope of the question to make it more manageable.

However, despite this there remain a number of ambiguous and vague terms:

- artificial intelligence: do we treat this as a phrase, or two individual words? Both 'artificial' and 'intelligence' are vague, as they refer to a range of possibilities: we are dealing with degrees and kinds of artificiality and of intelligence, not specific versions of each, still less a single meaning. As a term, 'artificial intelligence' (AI) has more of a case for being ambiguous: do we mean intelligence indistinguishable from that of a human (certainly not possible at the moment) or instead a more limited capacity for autonomous self-learning, or do we mean the ability to process new pieces of information using existing processes, as opposed to processing expected items of information using fixed mechanisms for response?

- beneficial: this is a vague term, as it refers to the production of a benefit, or good outcome, of something in general, in any number of different contexts. Why might artificial intelligence be a good thing for human beings, and what kind of good thing, or things, might it produce?

- humans: the final term in the question is also ambiguous. What do we mean by 'humans'? The whole human species, or human beings living now, in a particular place and culture?

Removing vagueness and ambiguity

The most obvious method for removing the vagueness and ambiguity we have just described is to make clear what each term means. One way of doing that is simply to use a dictionary to discover how it defines them. Taking the three terms we have just identified from our question, this is what the *Shorter Oxford English Dictionary* tells us about 'artificial intelligence': 'the capacity of a machine to simulate or surpass intelligent human behaviour'.

This definition is helpful in reducing some of the areas of ambiguity we identified. 'Intelligence' is 'intelligent human behaviour', and 'artificial' is defined as a machine's capacity 'to simulate or surpass' that behaviour of intelligent humans. The term is not completely clarified because the dictionary seems to offer two distinct alternatives for 'artificial': simulating (giving the appearance of) or surpassing (being even more than) 'intelligent human behaviour'. That focus on behaviour also suggests that intelligence should be measured in terms of how it makes us act, rather than actually what it is.

If we turn to 'beneficial', however, the dictionary definition is much less straightforward:

1 (a) of benefit, advantageous (b) lucrative, bringing pecuniary benefit

2 actively kind

3 of or pertaining to a church benefice

KEY TERMS

stipulated definition: a definition that is declared, or stipulated, as the one that should be used for the context being described

expert definition: a definition from an expert in the field which represents a meaning for the term based on specialist knowledge

clarification by contrast: clarification of the meaning of a term by contrasting it with what it is not, in order to narrow down the possible range of things it could be understood as

clarification by example: clarification of a term by giving examples of what it is, or what it is not, in order to help the reader understand what is being described

dictionary definition: the definition of a term found in a dictionary, describing its usage in ordinary language

4 (Law) of, pertaining to, or having the use or benefit of property; (of a trust) in which legal entitlement to property is vested in a trustee, who is obliged to hold the property for the benefit of the person or persons entitled under the trust

Clearly, most of these definitions are themselves either obscure or not relevant to this context, so would need to be excluded. These would include definitions 3 and 4 because they specifically apply to church regulations and the law of property trusts, neither of which applies here. Definition 2 does not fit the sense of the question or the situation. This leaves the first definition, which does not seem to move us much further forward, apart from confirming that it relates to benefits and advantages, and suggesting that one specific advantage might be pecuniary, or in other words relating to money.

Already, we are having to use other methods to clarify exactly what we mean. First of all, we have had to **stipulate**, or set out, which dictionary definitions we would or would not use. Effectively, we are telling the reader of our essay that they should understand the term in some ways but not in others for the purposes of our discussion. In the case of 'artificial intelligence' in particular, a definition from an **expert** in the field (here, a source who is a computer expert) would help us to decide which definition of artificial intelligence we should use.

Sometimes the best definitions do not require reference to an external source at all. One way to focus ourselves on what is 'beneficial', for instance, is to draw a **contrast** between that and what we do not want to look at. Something that is beneficial is not harmful, so we are interested in deciding whether artificial intelligence is not harmful to humans. We can then give **examples** of what specific benefits or harms might be caused by it. Here, these might come from examples contained in evidence given by sources we find in our research.

ACTIVITY 4.08

Consider again the question we have been clarifying in this section:

- Is artificial intelligence beneficial for humans?

How would you clarify each of its terms? Which of the methods we have outlined would you use, and why?

Discussion point

How do you think this clarification would help you in researching and writing an essay in response to this question?

The purpose of clarification and questioning

The most important thing to remember about clarification is that it has a purpose in helping you to research and write an essay in response to the question. You are not just aiming to be clear about the meanings of each of the words in the title, you also need to know:

- the main focus of the question
- the limits of the question: what it does and does not include
- how you might define and build up different perspectives in response to the question
- how you might start to come to a conclusion in response to the question.

Clarification is part of the process of being inquisitive about your research and writing: asking questions that will guide your selection of sources and your construction of an argument. This will bring your question into line with the issue, the debate, themes and perspectives, as well as the purpose of a Global Perspectives & Research essay which demonstrates the skills associated with the Critical Path.

In the next chapter, we will discuss in detail how you might actually go about writing each part of your essay, but that will be closely informed by what we have established here.

Summary

In this chapter we have:

- considered the role of reflection in essay writing

- defined what an essay is and considered the differences between essays in other subjects and Global Perspectives & Research

- refined topics into more focused issues about which essays can be written

- organised issues into opposing perspectives using themes

- identified the most appropriate question types to use for essays

- analysed and evaluated effective essay questions against a range of criteria

- explored a range of approaches to clarifying the terms used in questions in order to focus your thinking and arguments.

Successful essays are the result of planning as much as writing (which is dealt with in Chapter 5). This chapter has provided some guidance for that process by considering how topics can be refined into issues and organised into perspectives using themes so that your essays are focused in an appropriate way for the Global Perspectives & Research course. Effective questions are also crucial to successful essays, and the remainder of the chapter has been dedicated to methods for developing questions which work well, and organising your thoughts further by clarifying terms to remove vagueness and ambiguity.

Deconstruction

Reconstruction

Reflection

Practising question planning

This section of the chapter is divided into three: firstly, establishing work with planning essay questions, secondly, developing the skill of question planning and finally, enhancing question planning and writing. Each section is designed to build on the one before. You can either work through each section in turn or choose the section that you feel is at the most appropriate level for you. You should see a progression of difficulty through the three levels, but they are also linked in this chapter to the distinctive skills we have established.

These sections use a variety of topics from the Cambridge International AS & A Level Global Perspectives & Research syllabus. Some are specified, but in other cases you are invited to choose your own. This is intended to be part of your progression towards working independently as you choose essay topics of your own, and construct your own questions.

Establishing work with planning essay questions

Read through the following list of possible essay questions. For each one, assess whether it would make a suitable title for a successful Global Perspectives & Research essay:

1 International Aid Agencies

2 Is renewable energy worth the investment it requires, and will it work as a replacement for fossil fuels?

3 Do modern banking institutions strengthen or undermine societies?

4 Explain why companies who pollute the environment should be responsible for cleaning it up.

5 Should we protect endangered cultures?

6 Does France benefit from being a member of NATO?

7 Should the arts be publicly funded?

8 Why is it important to protect biodiversity in rainforests?

For each of these, you should consider whether:

- it specifies an issue, and focuses on a debate between different perspectives organised by themes
- it allows for the deconstruction and reconstruction of opposing arguments and perspectives
- it is possible to reach a conclusion in response to the question that is supported by reasons
- it is one question, not two or more
- it is not too broad to successfully answer, but is also global in scope.

Developing work with planning essay questions

Read through the following list of effective essay questions. For each, list the terms you think should be clarified, and explain how and why you would clarify them using the methods of clarification listed in this chapter:

1 Does the state need to censor the media?

2 Is marine bioprospecting ethical?

3 Should creationism be taught in publicly funded schools?

4 Do the Olympic Games benefit the host population?

Enhancing work with planning essay questions

Use the skills you have developed in this chapter to write at least three essay questions of your own. For each one, you should:

- choose a topic
- select an issue from within it
- construct a suitable question format
- identify opposing themes and perspectives.

When you have written your essay questions, you should clarify the terms in them using the methods described in this chapter.

If you wish, you could also make a list of sources you have found (using the methods described in Chapter 3) which would be suitable for inclusion in each of your questions.

Chapter 5
Communication: writing the essay

Learning aims

By the end of this chapter, you should be able to:

- effectively structure an essay in response to a question
- write effective introductions
- introduce and present different perspectives effectively in an essay
- write effective conclusions to essays
- cite and reference sources using recognised conventions.

This chapter will support you with writing essays. Chapters 4 and 5 cover different aspects of researching and writing essays.

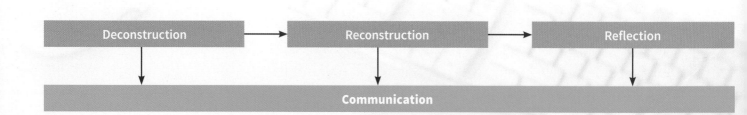

Deconstruction	Reconstruction	Reflection
Communication		

Introduction

This chapter focuses squarely on communication. As we saw in Chapter 1, communication is a stage of the Critical Path, but unlike deconstruction, reconstruction and reflection it cannot be placed as a single stage in a sequence of actions we go through when reading sources, engaging with other perspectives and making supported arguments of our own. Instead, it informs every one of these stages as the set of skills we need when presenting what we have done to others.

Communication can take place in both written and spoken forms, and in Global Perspectives & Research we are interested in developing our competence in doing both. Chapter 7 has lots of advice on communicating orally in formal academic presentations, so in this chapter we will be discussing how to communicate in writing in essays. In Chapter 4, we examined what an essay is, the specific expectations of a Global Perspectives & Research essay, how you can best identify a suitable focus for your essay and how to construct a question which will allow you to produce an effective essay in response.

5.01 Structuring your essay

In Chapter 4, we looked at the importance of starting your planning for an essay by selecting a topic from the Cambridge International AS & A Level Global Perspectives & Research syllabus, then identifying a specific issue within this before using the Global Perspectives & Research themes to develop globally contrasting perspectives on the issue using your research so that you can come to a supported conclusion. We then examined in some detail how to construct a question which will effectively allow you to do that.

It is not, however, just the essay question which needs to reflect that purpose but also the structure of the essay itself. The structure of a piece of writing is the sequence and organisation of the parts from which it is made up. We have already looked at structure in Chapter 2 when we identified the structure of arguments we find in sources and evaluated their strengths and weaknesses using deconstruction. This showed that arguments are not just made up of reasons followed by a conclusion, but can also have separate lines of argument – different types, or directions, of argument – which each have their own intermediate conclusion leading to the final, or main, conclusion. The strength of an argument's structure depends on how well each line of argument supports its own intermediate conclusion and how well each intermediate conclusion complements the others in supporting the main conclusion. Just like a well-made building, each part needs to perform its own function well, and everything needs to fit together to make a whole without excessively large gaps.

As we saw in Chapter 4, successful Global Perspectives & Research essays are also arguments, so they need to be well structured in the same way. This means that they will contain:

- a main conclusion
- reasons and evidence
- different lines of argument.

They will also, ideally, introduce that argument by clarifying and **contextualising** the question. This will ensure that what you write addresses your question and you have shown why your question is important and interesting to answer.

Each line of argument should also be related to one of the perspectives you have researched, so that you can organise your presentation of them before coming to a judgement of your own.

KEY TERM

contextualisation: the background and significance of a question, established before embarking on an argument

ACTIVITY 5.01

Consider an essay question you are currently working on, or a question you developed or identified from doing the activities at the end of Chapter 4.

Once you have your question, discuss and make notes in response to the following points:

1. What are the important terms in your question and how would you clarify them?
2. Why is your question important and interesting to answer?
3. Summarise two or more perspectives you have researched in response to your question. What does each of them conclude, what reasons and evidence do they use to support their arguments, and how strong do you think these are?
4. At this stage, what do you think your main conclusion should contain? This will include a judgement, or answer, in response to your question, and the main reasons and evidence which you think justify it. You should also add any ideas for further research you might want to do on this topic, and why that would be useful.

You now have the material you need to start writing your essay following the guidance given in the rest of this chapter.

Discussion point

It is important to bear in mind that the Critical Path is interconnected. This means that you cannot start to produce your writing until you have undertaken your research and organised your findings into a question and perspectives.

Take this opportunity to discuss with other students how they have answered these questions, and what their understanding is of organising their question and perspectives to prepare for writing.

Sequencing your ideas

KEY TERM

thesis-antithesis-synthesis: approach to essay writing which involves establishing a perspective, exploring one that opposes it, then reaching a synthesis, or combination, of the two

Once you are clear on your question, have researched your perspectives and have considered a possible conclusion, you will need to consider the sequence into which this should be organised. One well-established method is known as **thesis-antithesis-synthesis**. This sequence of thought originated with the 18th-century German philosophers Immanuel Kant and Johann Fichte, but is now commonly used to describe the structure of argument most appropriate for academic essay writing, and is also particularly suitable for essays you might write as part of the Global Perspectives & Research course. It is usually explained for essay writing in the following way:

1. The **thesis** is first developed as an idea, argument or group of similar arguments.
2. The **antithesis** is then set out as ideas or arguments which oppose the thesis.
3. A **synthesis** is then proposed which combines elements of the thesis and antithesis, and attempts to resolve any differences between them.

For essays written as part of the Critical Path, the sequence of thesis, antithesis and synthesis might work like this:

1. Set out the arguments and evidence for one of your perspectives (the thesis), referring to the sources which support it and evaluating their strengths and weaknesses.
2. Set out the arguments and evidence for the main perspective which opposes the perspective from the first stage (the antithesis), referring to the sources which support it and evaluating their strengths and weaknesses.
3. Suggest a synthesis. This might be a direct combination of the first and second perspectives, or a third perspective which includes elements of both. It should be supported by arguments and evidence.

Communication

This sequence makes up the **main body** of your essay. It allows perspectives to be grouped and contrasted in a way which also shows how your line of argument is developing. It should still be preceded by an **introduction** and followed by the **conclusion**.

Modelling essay structures

This section has **modelled** some approaches to structuring essays, but these are not the only ways of doing it. Remember that one of the meanings of an essay is an experiment in writing. It is up to you to find your own way of organising your material in a way that best suits the question you have decided to answer and the perspectives you have researched.

Whatever you do develop has to respect the principles of the Critical Path and the expectations of a Global Perspectives & Research essay which were outlined in Chapter 4. Briefly, these are:

- Your essay will be an argument, not another kind of writing.
- You will use evidence to support your reasons.
- Your evidence will come from a range of different sources.
- Your essay will be focused on a specific issue, and that issue will be based on the topics listed in the Cambridge International AS & A Level Global Perspectives & Research syllabus.
- It will be organised around debates between opposing points of view, rather than only acknowledging one approach to the issue.
- Your essay will therefore respond to a question which is focused on a global debate around a specific issue.
- Essays written for Global Perspectives & Research will always be reflective, consciously considering the similarities and differences between perspectives and weighing them up at the end in order to reach a conclusion.

The structure of thesis, antithesis and synthesis we have already suggested, and the expectations of a Global Perspectives & Research essay we have just listed, are therefore patterns for you to measure your own writing against. In doing so you will need to ask yourself how your own writing is similar or different to these guidelines, and reflect yourself on how you want to develop it in response.

ACTIVITY 5.02

Take the idea for an essay you were working with for Activity 5.01 and consider how closely its structure matches this model. What would be its best shape, and do any of these suggestions help? In particular, try organising the sources, arguments and evidence you have collected into the thesis-antithesis-synthesis structure.

In the next three sections some more detailed models will be explored for each of the main stages of an essay: the introduction to the essay itself, the introduction of the different perspectives in the main body of the essay and the essay's conclusion. Once again, you may want to use this to consider your own essay writing and how you might develop aspects of your style and approach.

Remember that however you structure your Global Perspectives & Research essay, you will need to limit its length to 2,000 words. This does not include the bibliography at the end (which is discussed further in Section 5.05) but does include everything from the beginning of the first paragraph to the end of the last. This means that your planned material should not extend beyond this, but equally should not significantly undercut it, as otherwise you will be losing opportunities to explore perspectives, present arguments and evidence and develop your conclusion.

Discussion point

Talk with your teacher or other students about how you will combine detail with writing to a strict word limit, and any practical strategies you have to achieve this. Do you know how to get a word count using your word processing software, and how to just count the words from the beginning of the first paragraph to the end of the last?

5.02 Effective introductions

As we have already seen, the purpose of an introduction to an essay is to clarify terms in the question, provide some context for its significance and produce a focus for the argument which will be explored.

Communication

The following introduction, for a Global Perspectives & Research essay with the title 'Is sustainability more important than the need for global development?', does this effectively:

> Humans have been aware for centuries that the ways in which we use natural resources in many areas of the world to support our lifestyles is a threat to our well-being and even existence. As we, however, move towards an exponential population growth that has already reached over seven billion people, the idea of *sustainability is increasingly marginalised in favour of a concern with combating disease or poverty*. But sustainability was never meant to be an obstacle to development, rather the holistic means to an outcome which is acceptable to all. *The phrase 'sustainable development' should be defined as an approach to seeing the globally interconnected economy of the world in conjunction with society and the environment in which we reside*. Successful development allows for simultaneous economic, social and environmental advances on a global scale, where progress in one of these does not compromise the other two.

The writer of this essay uses this introductory paragraph to serve three main functions, and weaves them together into a seamless whole:

1 It begins with the context of the question (marked in green), explaining the situation which makes the relationship between sustainability and development important: humans' use of natural resources to develop our lifestyles potentially threatens our well-being and sustainable existence on the planet.

2 Then, with the text marked in blue, it turns to the focus of the arguments that will be made in the essay. This consists of an argument and a counterargument which can be summarised in the following way:

    1 Using development to provide solutions for poverty or disease now is more important than creating sustainable solutions for the longer term.

        1.1 Sustainability does not oppose development but actually takes account of all factors (is holistic) and so provides an outcome which will be acceptable to everyone's interests, both in the short and longer term.

These have the potential to be used to organise the perspectives which will be researched, presented and evaluated in the rest of the essay.

3 As it provides context and focuses the argument, the introduction also clarifies key terms from the question using the methods of clarification outlined in Chapter 4

4 These are shown in italics. First, *sustainability* is clarified by contrast with combating disease and poverty, which are examples of development. This initial definition is then challenged, however, with an alternative which combines development and sustainability: sustainable development is stipulated as development which is economic, social and environmental, without losing any of these aspects.

The introduction therefore starts with the context so that the reader has the essential background information they need to make sense of the question and the argument. It then sets out the focus for the argument it will make, including the relationship between the thesis and the antithesis: the two main perspectives the essay will explore. As part of this, it clarifies the key terms in the question, and links this clarification to the perspectives and the argument.

It is important to realise here that successful clarification uses the *most appropriate* method to make the key terms clear (not just a dictionary definition, for example) and *links* the clarification to the summary of the argument, so that they support each other and clarification is not something separate.

Communication

ACTIVITY 5.03

Assess the following introduction. The question is 'Is economic or social success equivalent to personal happiness?'.

a Can you identify where this introduction contextualises its argument?

b What is the focus of the argument that will be made?

c How does it clarify terms?

d Using these criteria, how successful is this introduction?

It is a common belief in the world today that in order to achieve happiness, one needs to conform to social standards and be economically successful. But is this the case? Happiness seems a straightforward idea, but is actually a complex mixture of sensory pleasure and satisfaction with life. Some studies of happiness argue that personal happiness is based on a person's perception of their own economic prosperity. In contrast, other research, based on psychology, claims that we cannot produce a universal definition of happiness because how it is viewed is culturally dependent. Before we can reach a clear understanding of how happiness functions across the globe, it is necessary to decide whether life satisfaction is always reliant on success.

When assessing the strengths and weaknesses of this introduction, we can note that it does include the three elements of contextualisation, focusing the argument around opposing

Reflection: As with the previous example, this introduction starts with contextualisation, suggesting that the link between social conformity, economic success and happiness is a commonly held belief. This helps the reader to understand the relevance of the question and have a point of contact for approaching it. The rhetorical question, 'But is this the case?', does not require a response but identifies where the debate will be. Two perspectives are then established in order to focus that debate and the arguments which will be organised later in the essay. The first is that happiness is always the same and always based on economic prosperity. The second, on the other hand, is that happiness cannot be universally defined and is dependent on the cultural context. Alongside this, the introduction also clarifies some of the key terms, defining happiness as a 'complex' mix by contrast with a 'straightforward' definition.

perspectives and clarification of key terms. These elements are also linked to each other and a debate is clearly established. However, the introduction also makes a number of assumptions that might be harder to justify: is it really a 'common belief' that happiness is linked to social conformity and economic success? Who thinks this? Happiness is not necessarily 'straightforward' either, and the assertion that it is a 'complex mixture' also needs to be supported by evidence.

How might you develop this introduction to make it even more effective?

5.03 The main body of the essay

After the introduction, you will move into the main body of the essay. As we have already seen, this is the place where you introduce, develop and contrast the different perspectives. Here are some examples of the introduction of perspectives in Global

Perspectives & Research essays. Each extract has a number of differences as well as features in common:

Extract A: 'Should English be adopted as the global language of instruction in education systems?'

Those who are against English as the language of instruction hold this position because of the risks it presents to their own language and culture, and because it would make the world more homogenous. A number of literary writers and post-colonial theorists also connect the spread of English to the destructive colonial regime of the British, and see it as an example of neo-imperialism.

Extract B: 'Do the dangers of artificial intelligence outweigh the benefits?'

Artificial intelligence can be seen as a hidden but extremely dangerous problem which will suddenly reveal itself at some point in the future. Because AI is incorporated into every aspect of life, this will have an impact on everyone in society once it emerges. Elaine Feng argues that the most significant negative consequences of AI will be seen first in the developing world.

Extract C: 'Is the death penalty ethically acceptable?'

Grace A. Babbage claims that the death penalty is a matter of human rights and not just a form of punishment. In her article, 'The death penalty: A worldwide debate', she cites the ways in which the capital punishment laws of the United States have compromised human rights. To support her perspective, Babbage uses numerous sources of information.

Each extract has a number of differences as well as features in common:

- Extract A begins by describing the perspective which opposes English as the global language of instruction in school in general, and then lists groups of sources with some of their reasons for arguing this.
- Extract B describes in general the perspective which sees artificial intelligence as being more dangerous than safe, and then summarises an argument from one specific source within this perspective.
- Extract C starts with one specific source that argues against the death penalty on the ethical basis of human rights and then turns to wider sources of evidence which that source uses to support its argument.

These differences show contrasts in how each essay chooses to navigate the perspective it is introducing. Some engage with the perspective as a whole in different ways before moving to specific arguments, but others either start with the whole perspective then move to an individual source, or begin with the individual source as a starting point for exploring the larger perspective.

ACTIVITY 5.04

Write about 60 words introducing the first perspective for your planned essay question. This is about the same as each of the extracts given above.

Choose one of the methods discussed for structuring it: moving from perspective to arguments, from perspective to sources, or from source to perspective.

You may find it helpful to use three colours to highlight where you address sources, perspectives and arguments.

What this shows is that you have a lot of flexibility when it comes to introducing and developing each of your perspectives. The starting point matters less than what you eventually cover, provided that you have a clear order in mind. When considering what should be in the main body of the essay, it is helpful to think of a minimum set of ingredients which it should contain. These are:

- two perspectives: these should provide contrasting answers to the question you have asked yourself

- analysis and evaluation of your perspectives, breaking them down and weighing up their strengths and weaknesses as responses to your question

- individual sources you can identify which support each of your perspectives by providing arguments and evidence for them

- analysis and evaluation of each of the sources, which could cover the structure of their argument, the evidence they use and where they come from.

Chapters 2–4 contain detailed information on each of these ingredients, and how they should be prepared. When you come to write your essay, you are focused instead on the order in which you should put them together in order to explore different perspectives on your question and reach an overall judgement.

Topic sentences

Topic sentences are an important tool in essays to show the reader what the focus of each paragraph is. You can also use them to organise the development of your perspectives in each paragraph.

Read again the three extracts from the beginning of this section (A, B and C). In particular, look at the first sentence of each. These are listed again for you below:

a) Those who are against English as the language of instruction hold this position because of the risks it presents to their own language and culture, and because it would make the world more homogenous.

b) Artificial intelligence can be seen as a hidden but extremely dangerous problem which will suddenly reveal itself at some point in the future.

c) Grace A. Babbage claims that the death penalty is a matter of human rights and not just a form of punishment.

KEY TERM

topic sentence:
the first sentence of a paragraph which summarises its content, including the argument it presents

All three of these sentences are effective topic sentences because they are located at the start of the paragraph and use this to summarise its topic. They do this by:

- describing what the paragraph will contain
- summarising the argument that will be presented in the paragraph.

Using topic sentences is useful because it helps your reader to navigate your essay by seeing what each paragraph will contain, but it also disciplines you as a writer: each paragraph should contain just what is indicated in the topic sentence and nothing else. Using topic sentences properly means that each of your paragraphs will be focused and not contain any material that is irrelevant to what you want to say.

ACTIVITY 5.05

Read the following two paragraphs from Global Perspectives & Research essays. In each case the topic sentence has been removed. Write a topic sentence to replace this which fulfils the two purposes of a topic sentence (describing what the paragraph contains and summarising the argument that is presented in it).

A: 'Would the world be a better place if we all spoke one language?'

. . . The 6 billion people on this planet need to be able to communicate with each other in order to be economically secure and to peacefully co-exist. They also claim that it would be much easier to travel and conduct business if we did not have to contend with foreign languages. Scientists and scholars would also be able to work much easier together if there were one universal language of learning. Finally many of the misunderstandings and prejudices of the world would be avoided if we could understand each other better.

B: 'Does globalisation benefit less economically developed countries?'

. . . They claim that the freer trade, especially in agricultural goods, has worked to 'threaten or destroy the livelihoods of millions of farmers' and to keep people in poverty. This is because cheaper agricultural imports can be bought in such developing countries, thus decreasing the competitiveness of domestic agricultural produce, threatening the wellbeing of local farmers. This is despite the fact that the supporters of globalisation contend it has also led to the opening of many other markets for under-developed countries.

Reflection: The first extract, in response to the question 'Would the world be a better place if we all spoke one language?', focuses entirely on arguments that it would if this was the case. Furthermore, all of these arguments, from the first sentence onwards, are based on its benefits for communication. For example, communication is claimed to benefit everyone economically and make everyone more secure, and more effective communication is also said to have benefits for travel, business, science and scholarship, and in resolving 'misunderstandings and prejudice'. The second sentence also refers to a group of people supporting these arguments as 'they'. An effective topic sentence would identify this as a group of communication arguments supporting a single global language and say who 'they' are. You will have come up with your own; the original topic sentence did this as follows: 'Supporters of a single global language argue for greater facility of communication among and between the world's peoples'.

The second extract again takes one side and one aspect of the debate in response to the question 'Does globalisation benefit less economically developed countries?'. It focuses on why the free trade aspect of globalisation, where there are reduced restrictions on trade between countries, harms less economically developed countries. It does so by presenting this argument from one source and assessing its strengths and weaknesses by providing additional reasons for the claim that free trade has destroyed the livelihoods of millions of farmers, but also raising a possible counter-argument in the final sentence (liberalising, or freeing, trade has opened up some markets for less developed countries). An effective topic sentence should therefore identify where the argument being quoted has come from and summarise where in the debate it is located. Again, you will have thought of your own version of this, but the original to which you can compare your own effort was 'Critics of globalisation, like the British charity ActionAid, argue that trade liberalisation has harmed developing countries'. The quotation is from a source authored by the charity ActionAid.

Argument signposts and content words

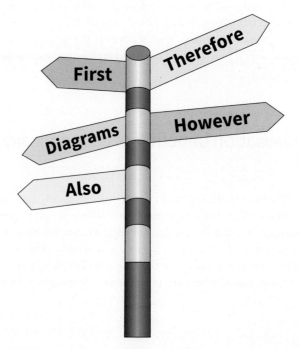

As well as summarising the content and argument of each of your paragraphs, you can also use your topic sentences – and other parts of your essay – to create **signposts** for your reader. These are especially useful in the main body of the essay, as they help readers to work out where they are in the structure and to navigate their way through your presentation of each of your perspectives.

We first came across argument signposts in Chapter 2, where we called them argument indicators: the words in other people's arguments which show where the conclusions and reasons are located. As a reminder, here are some examples:

- Conclusion indicators: *therefore, accordingly, as a result, this means that*
- Reason indicators: *first, second, third, because*

Argument indicators show the key locations in your argument. These include where you are reaching a final or intermediate conclusion, where you are giving reasons, and how many reasons are attached to a specific point. Other kinds of signposts also help your reader to see where they are in your essay. One important purpose is to show when you are switching from one side of your debate to another. Words which do this include:

- however
- on the other hand
- in contrast.

Equally, a signpost can indicate that you are continuing to travel in the same direction, and that the next claim, piece of evidence or source builds on what you have just said. Here are some examples of words and phrases which do this:

- furthermore
- in addition
- also.

Finally, another important method for focusing each of your sentences is to use **content words** to highlight the key content of each paragraph. We saw this in the previous section on topic sentences. There, the first example in the activity used the word 'communication' and the second example used the phrase 'trade liberalisation'. Both of these highlight not the overall topic of the essay, but the specific aspect that is being dealt with in that section. Placing these in topic sentences and returning to them in each section makes it clear what your focus is and helps you to develop your argument in the same direction without including anything irrelevant.

It is very important to help your reader by using signposts and content words. They make your essay much easier to read and also support you in producing an argument which is as well-shaped and supported as those you have been trying to find in the sources you have used. If you use them effectively, it will be very clear what the main concern of each perspective is, where you are switching between perspectives, when you are giving reasons and drawing conclusions, and how all of this relates to your question.

KEY TERM

content word: word in an essay which shows the key content which is being focused on in each paragraph

---

ACTIVITY 5.06

Make a list of the key content words in your own essay. You may choose to make a mind-map of them based on the research you have done. Try to ensure that your final choices reflect your question and perspectives.

Once you have already written your essay, try putting the text into Worldle (www.wordle.net/create). This will make a 'word cloud' with the words occurring most often appearing largest. Do the largest words coincide with your key content words? If not, why not?

5.04 Effective conclusions

Conclusions are an essential part of any argument, and this is no less true of the argument you make in response to your question in your essay. This means that your essay must end with a final judgement which answers your question. Here are final judgements for some of the questions we have already looked at:

- 'Do the dangers of artificial intelligence outweigh the benefits?': 'Thus, the benefits associated with artificial intelligence far outweigh the dangers.'
- 'Is the death penalty ethically acceptable?': 'Although capital punishment should be ethically acceptable, there needs to be international reform concerning its use to ensure it is ethically applied.'

ACTIVITY 5.07

For each of these questions, consider how you would answer it and write that final judgement as a single sentence.

- Does globalisation benefit less economically developed countries?
- Would the world be a better place if we all spoke one language?
- Should English be adopted as the global language of instruction in education systems?
- Is economic or social success equivalent to personal happiness?

Once you have done this, consider a question of your own you have been planning (either as an activity for Chapter 4, or one from your own research in class). Write down how, at the moment, you would answer it in one sentence.

Reflection: Although we have looked at these questions earlier in the chapter, you may well feel that you do not have enough information to reach a judgement you are confident about. You may also feel that you would like to say more to justify your answer. Restricting your final judgement to a single sentence is a good discipline because it is more likely to make you come to a firm answer. However, you will also still need to justify what you say in your conclusion, and it is on this that the rest of this section is focused.

Justifying final judgements

Conclusions are a two-stage process: the final judgement and your justification of that final judgement. The conclusion is the place in which you should gather together the key arguments and evidence from each perspective and make clear how you are using these to support your final judgement.

If you are following the thesis-antithesis-synthesis structure for your essay, your conclusion might use the synthesis of perspectives, combining the most convincing elements of each, as the first stage of the conclusion. Having weighed up each perspective in turn, you can then use this stage to test out ideas before reaching your final judgement.

Discussion point

How have you chosen to justify your final judgement in your conclusion? Share the approach you have taken with other students, and discuss similarities and differences.

Communication

Whichever approach you take, you should aim to write at least one paragraph summarising the arguments and evidence from each perspective you will use in reaching your conclusion, and then a further paragraph which refers back to these and contains your final judgement, which may be one or two sentences and is a direct answer to your question.

ACTIVITY 5.08

Look again at the question of your own which you were considering for Activity 5.05 and the one-sentence final judgement you have written for it. Now list up to four reasons or pieces of evidence which directly support that judgement.

Once you have done this, match the reasons to the perspectives you have researched. Do they come from one perspective only, or more than one perspective? What does this tell you about the judgement you have reached?

Reflecting on further research

It might surprise you to consider that your final judgement should not be the last word of your essay. As part of a process of research into a question, your essay of 2,000 words is a snapshot of the argument and conclusions you have achieved over a certain length of time and within a particular, limited space. Part of your judgement is to be able to identify what more might be said. Which relevant perspectives have you not been able to explore? What other evidence, if used, might make a difference to your conclusions? Perhaps it is even the case that the research you have done suggests that formulating the question in a slightly different way might produce a more illuminating answer.

There are three ways in which you might deal with further research in your essay, each one better than the last:

1 You might not mention possible further research at all.
2 You might mention it, but do so just by listing the additional areas, sources, arguments or evidence you would want to look at.
3 You might not only list the things you would want to look at, but also explain why these would be helpful for your research into that question, and begin to consider how doing so might change, confirm or develop your findings.

Another way in which to think about these alternatives is to consider which one is most useful. Evaluating why you might want to carry out a specific piece of further research is the best way of ensuring that you are embarking on the most useful further path for answering your question or exploring that issue, and justifying that decision. Thinking about the next step, or further avenues for reading and research, is also a very good habit to get into. It is a useful way of thinking if you plan to continue your studies at university and also for any research you might do towards your research report, which is discussed in Chapter 9.

Discussion point

What else do you think you would like to research which you have not already covered in the work you have done for your essay?

Discuss this with other students and also consider why you would want to look at these areas.

5.05 Citation and referencing

When you write essays, you are entering into a form of public dialogue. Even though it may seem that you are only being read by your fellow students, your teacher and an examiner you have never met, by writing arguments for others you are already entering into a conversation where you set out your ideas and evidence and they can use them to respond and develop arguments of their own.

Because of this, it is very important that you are able to demonstrate which are your claims, and which lines of reasoning and evidence are used from elsewhere, and where they can be found. This is done through **citation** and **referencing**. These are consistent ways of showing where you are using material from other sources and where your reader can find those sources for themselves.

Citation and referencing have three main purposes:

KEY TERMS

citation: a notation of where you have used material from someone else in your own writing

referencing: giving details of how to locate sources you have cited

- They avoid plagiarism (the presenting of other people's work as your own) by clearly referencing the sources you have made use of in your work.

- They help your own organisation by enabling you to keep track of the sources you have collected in the course of your research. Proper citation and referencing start with effectively recording where each of the sources you have researched comes from, so that you can find it again, using the note-taking techniques outlined in Chapter 3.

- They help research and enquiry more generally. If you list your sources in a standard format that other researchers can interpret, with all the information they require to make sense of and, if necessary, find your sources for themselves, they can corroborate your findings and make use of your work as a starting point for work of their own. Even though you are an A Level student now, you are already a researcher and should think of yourself as part of a research community.

Reflection: Why do you think citation and referencing are important for you and your writing? Consider what you feel the most useful factor is for you.

Citation

Citation is as straightforward as identifying which author or publication has made a claim or presented evidence which you wish to make use of in your own argument. For example:

> *'Pharmaceuticals: A Gathering Storm' in The Economist* uses the example of Thailand to make the case that ignoring patent restrictions on drugs may actually be harmful for a country in the long term.

> *Kenan Malik,* however, has a contrasting argument on the topic of endangered language preservation. He argues *in an essay entitled 'Let Them Die'* that endangered languages should not be preserved.

In each case the citation of sources is highlighted in italics. The author's name (or in the case of *The Economist*, where articles are unsigned, the publication) is included along with the title of the source in the text of the essay itself, and integrated into the writer's sentences. Here, the arguments from the sources are **paraphrased** – they are cited in the essay writer's own words, rather than being the words from the source. This does not make it any less important to show that the argument itself does come from that source, and not the writer's own ideas.

KEY TERMS

paraphrase: material from a source rephrased in your own words

verbatim citation: the exact words from a source, indicated by quotation marks

Where words from the source are used directly, we call this **verbatim citation**. The second of the two essays quoted above does this as it continues:

> Malik's main claim is that the point of a language is to 'enable communication' and therefore it is not necessary to keep something that is only spoken by a relatively small number of people.

The words which come directly from Malik's source are placed in quotation marks to make this clear, even though they are incorporated into the writer's own sentence. When citing verbatim, it is important to integrate what is quoted into your own writing. This might be by only quoting a few words and incorporating them into your sentences. Alternatively, you might use a longer quotation and place it at the end of sentence, with a colon indicating that the quotation is to follow:

> His main claim seems more surprising: most languages die out 'because the native speakers yearn for a better life'.

Finally, especially if you want to quote a sentence or more from the source, you can use indented quotations. The quotations in this book are mainly indented, such as the examples above. They are set further to the right than your main text in a paragraph of their own, and omit quotation marks.

Referencing

Everything you cite in your essay must also be linked to a consistent system of referencing. This is a standard way of recording who wrote each source, where it is from, when it was written and how it was published. The reason this information should be recorded is to enable your reader to locate the source for themselves, either by searching on the internet

or in a library catalogue, and if they wish to read it for themselves or make use of it to check, challenge or develop your argument. Utilising a system of referencing in this way not only demonstrates that you have not engaged in plagiarism, it also enables you to join that community of readers and be part of that larger academic debate.

There is no specific method of referencing you need to use for Global Perspectives & Research essays. It is more important that you include enough information for your reader to be able to locate your sources and that you reference each source in the same way so that the information you provide is consistent. When you come to write your research report, depending on the subject of your research, some methods of referencing might be more useful than others. This is discussed in more detail in Chapter 9 along with details of different bibliographical systems. You should also bear in mind that your teacher may wish you to use a specific system of citation and referencing and will give you additional information about this. What is not an alternative is not to cite or reference at all, or to do so inconsistently.

One option you can use is a system called Harvard referencing. One advantage of this system is that it is simple to link your citations to your list of references in the **bibliography** at the end of your essay.

In the Harvard system, each cited source in the essay includes the surname of the author and the year in which the source was published, usually in parentheses (brackets). For example, you might write, 'Giles (2007) argues that the production of biofuels will help American agriculture'. If you cite a verbatim quotation, then include the page number in brackets: 'Smith calls this "trade liberalisation"' (2005, p. 22). If you use more than one source published by the same author in the same year, you can show which one is which by adding letters to the dates. For example, 'Jones argues that this is important for both fathers (2002a) and sons (2002b)'. This cites two sources both written by Jones in 2002. The one written first is labelled 2002a and the second is labelled 2002b.

At the end of your essay, you should include a bibliography of all the sources you have used. This should be in alphabetical order based on the author's surname. If articles within the source are unsigned, with no author name, then you should put the title first in alphabetical order.

This is how it would work for some specific sources using the Harvard system:

'The age of ethanol' (2010), *The Economist* (1 July 2010). Online. Available at: http://www.economist.com/node/16492491.

Berger, John (1972) *Ways of Seeing*. London: Penguin.

Giles, Jim (2007) 'Can biofuels rescue American prairies?', *New Scientist* (18 August 2007). Online. Available from: http://www.newscientist.com/article/mg19526173.400-can-biofuels-rescue-american-prairies.html.

The first reference in the list does not have an author name recorded, so gives the article title first. 'The', 'A' and 'An' do not count in alphabetical order, so it is listed under 'A' for 'age'. Following this comes the name of the publication, the date of the edition, 'Online' to indicate it was published on the internet and then at the end the URL so it can be located.

The second reference is a book with an author, so the author's name comes first. After the title of the book is the place of publication and the name of the publisher.

KEY TERM

bibliography: a list at the end of the essay of works that have been cited

The final reference is a journal article with an author published online. Because of this, the author's name comes first followed by the title of the article, the publication and the date of the edition.

In the Harvard system, the year of publication always follows the author or title in the bibliography and allows the reader to make a link between it and that author and year when it is cited in the text.

ACTIVITY 5.09

Gather together details of all the books you have researched for your essay and make a bibliography from them in Harvard style.

Check the accuracy of how you have set out your list against the examples listed above.

Summary

In this chapter we have:

- considered the importance of structure in writing an essay
- evaluated some effective methods for organising arguments and perspectives in essays
- identified and evaluated models for effective introductions
- practised writing introductions
- analysed how to introduce and present different perspectives effectively in an essay
- written effective conclusions to essays
- explained the importance of citation and referencing
- outlined how to cite and reference sources using recognised conventions.

This chapter has been all about supporting your writing of essays. In order to do that we have discussed the importance of structure, key content words, signposts and topic sentences, and given examples of effective ways of incorporating these into your writing. You have also had the chance to practise this in your own essays. Now that you have completed this chapter you should be ready to write your essay, and also have some effective skills towards writing your research report (Chapter 9).

Practising essay writing

This section of the chapter is divided into three: firstly, establishing work with essay writing, secondly, developing the skill of essay writing and finally, enhancing essay writing. Each section is designed to build on the one before. You can either work through each section in turn or choose the section that you feel is at the most appropriate level for you. However, you will notice that some of the questions are linked, so that you should attempt the question in a previous section before moving on to the connected question in the later section.

You should also see a progression of difficulty through the three levels, but they are also aligned in this chapter to the distinctive skills we have established.

These sections use a variety of topics from the Cambridge International AS & A Level Global Perspectives & Research syllabus. Some are specified, but in other cases you are invited to choose your own. This is intended to be part of your progression towards working independently as you choose essay topics of your own, and construct your own questions.

Establishing work with essay writing

1   Consider the following essay question:

'Should the English language be used as a global method of communication?'

The following list of arguments, found in a variety of sources researched by the student, were used in an essay answering the question:

*   Having one language for communication allows global trade to be more efficient.

*   Using English as an exclusive method of communication globally would cause other languages and their cultures to die out.

*   It is important to make a distinction between how we communicate in different contexts: nationally and locally.

*   The French language has a long history of being used for diplomatic communications in an international context.

*   The dominance of the English language is inappropriate in a century which is being defined by the rise of countries such as China.

*   The prevalence of American popular culture across the globe makes it appropriate to use English as a common method of communication.

Please place these into groups for how you would structure them into an essay. You might like to use the thesis-antithesis-synthesis structure. If you do, group them in this way:

a   arguments supporting your thesis (the first perspective you want to set out)

b   arguments against your thesis (those which come from a second perspective)

c   any arguments that combine both perspectives.

Are there any arguments in the list which are not relevant and should not be included?

2   Look at the argument signposts listed below. These are words and phrases which help your reader to navigate your essay by seeing the direction in which you are going. They are explained in more detail in Section 5.03.

*   firstly, because, furthermore, additionally, in contrast, this is reinforced by, therefore, finally, however, also, on the other hand, in conclusion, demonstrates that, hence, the reasons are

Organise them into the following categories:

* words and phrases introducing a conclusion
* words and phrases introducing a reason
* words and phrases showing that the next point builds on the last and the argument is moving in the same direction
* words and phrases showing that the next point contrasts with the last and the argument is moving in a different direction.

Developing work with essay writing

1 Look at the same essay question discussed in Question 1 of the previous section 'Establishing work with essay writing.' To get the most out of this question you will also have had to complete that one.

'Should the English language be used as a global method of communication?'

Given the arguments listed in Question 1 and your own existing awareness of this question, answer the following:

a What are the key terms in the question which should be clarified in the introduction?

b What background information, or context, would you want to give the reader of your essay about this issue?

c How would you summarise the thesis and antithesis in the introduction (using ideas from the two lists you created in the previous question)?

Once you have answered these, you may wish to write the introductory paragraph, using the examples in Section 5.02 as models. After you have written it, you can check your work against one of those models and the key criteria for an introduction, or ask someone else to check it.

2 Here is some more practice with topic sentences. Read this topic sentence below from a Global Perspectives & Research essay. Discuss and note down what you would expect the rest of the paragraph to contain.

> On the other hand, a range of human factors have been claimed to contribute to climate change.

Now read this paragraph which has had its topic sentence removed. Can you write a topic sentence which would fill the gap?

> . . . An example of this perspective can be seen in Ian Bremmer's article in *Time* magazine (2015), 'These Are the 5 Reasons Why the U.S. Remains the World's Only Superpower'. In this article Bremmer shows that the wealth of individual Chinese (GDP per capita) is much lower than in the United States, and that the US has a stronger military, more political influence, stronger technological research and a higher standard of living than China. Certainly when portrayed in this way the picture seems to be one of China as a struggling nation.

Finally, for each of the four example paragraphs you have been working with in this question, list what you think its key content words would be. These were explained in Section 5.03 and are words or phrases which summarise the main idea or focus in each of your paragraphs. They can be used most effectively in topic sentences, but can also be repeated through the paragraph and ensure that what you are writing is focused and relevant.

Enhancing work with essay writing

1 The final task in the 'Enhancing work' section in Chapter 4 asked you to make a list of the sources you had found for up to three essay questions of your own, using the research methods described in Chapter 3.

If you have not already got such a list, make one now for at least one question of your own.

Then, turn your list into a bibliography, using the exact Harvard format described in Section 5.05, or another standard system of referencing which your teacher has shared with you. You should note that a bibliography refers to all the sources you have looked at in your research, so not all of these will need to be cited in your essay. A list at the end of the essay of just the sources you have cited is called a 'List of Works Cited'.

2 Staying with the same question you selected for the first task in this section (and you now have a bibliography for), do the following two tasks:

   • Write the introductory paragraph for the essay and a plan following the thesis-antithesis-synthesis structure. This should also include ideas for the conclusion and further research.

   • Write the essay.

Chapter 6
Collaboration: introducing the team project

Learning aims

By the end of this chapter, you should be able to:

- understand the benefits and challenges involved in working together with others
- summarise the requirements of the team project
- work with members of your team to identify a local problem with global significance
- link the skills assessed by the team project to the Critical Path.

This chapter will support you with team projects. Chapters 6, 7 and 8 cover different aspects of team projects.

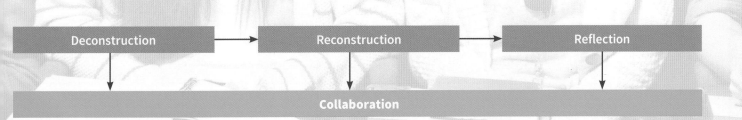

Deconstruction	Reconstruction	Reflection

Collaboration

Introduction

Collaboration, work performed together with other people, is an important skill within the Critical Path. It is likely that you will have worked in groups in at least some of the other subjects you are studying, and that you will also have done this at earlier stages of your education.

Listening to others, and taking account of their views, is especially valuable for students of Global Perspectives & Research. In previous chapters, you may have found it helpful to discuss ideas with other students to get their views and understand how different people approach the same issues. The third component of Global Perspectives & Research (and the final part required for the AS) is different in that it focuses specifically on developing team working and collaboration.

The team project is explored fully over Chapters 6–8. This chapter sets the scene by drawing attention to some of the benefits and challenges of working with other people, and then outlining precisely how the team project is organised and what it requires. Part of this includes the task you and your team will have to set for yourselves, which is different to the type of question asked in the written paper and essay. Having established the overall picture and set a starting point, Chapters 7 and 8 focus in on each of the assessed pieces you will produce: the individual presentation and the reflective paper.

6.01 Working with other people

We live in a connected world. Most of the ways in which we learn, work and access information and entertainment involve other people or groups of people. Some of these activities involve interacting with others at a distance involving social networks, voice calls, forums and group chat applications. Most of our interaction with groups still takes place in person, however. This might take place in our families, with groups of friends, as part of a team in the workplace or as a group of learners in education.

ACTIVITY 6.01

Here are some prompts to get you thinking about your experience of group work. For this activity, you may wish to consider them on your own before discussing them in groups. If you do talk them through with others it might also be interesting for you to reflect on whether this produces a different outcome.

1   List three or four groups you have been a member of in the past, are currently a part of or know about in any other way. These might be from a personal, educational or work context.

2   What are some of the advantages of working in groups?

3   Is there anything you find challenging or difficult about group work?

Once you have done this, focus on the groups you listed for the first prompt. For each of them, answer the following questions:

- Was the group deliberately created, or did it form spontaneously?
- Is there a group leader who gives instructions, or not?
- How many people are in the group, and what are the criteria for being a member?
- What is the purpose of the group, and what activities does it engage in?

For instance, possible advantages of group work might include getting a different perspective or new information on something you are studying, getting the opportunity to improve your communication skills or get to know new people, sharing your ideas with others, and getting better at managing time so you can co-ordinate work and deadlines with other people. On the other hand, these opportunities to develop new skills and ways of working can also be challenging, as they require growth and change. Building up any new skill will also inevitably mean that you may take the wrong direction or make mistakes. Working in a group may simply be something to which you are not accustomed. Perhaps you have not yet had a job where you are asked to work in teams, or your usual education setting may focus on individual working, or separate interactions between students and staff which do not involve peer conversations. There is a lot to think about here, and other people you know may have different ideas.

Equally, there is a surprising possible range of types of groups you may know about, or might even have been a member of yourself. These vary from the class you are in at school or college, following the Global Perspectives & Research course, to a group of staff working in a shop or even a group of friends who meet up socially.

The nature of groups

The questions you answered about your chosen groups are selected from a list of criteria for assessing groups developed by Tom Douglas, an academic studying the theory of how people work together in groups, in 1979. We can see how they are useful for categorising groups by applying them to these three examples:

Group 1: friendship group of 16- to 18-year-olds

- origin (how did it start?): formed spontaneously from students aged 16 to 18 years who met each other because they were in the same year group at school. Several members got to know each other to start with, and others have joined the group since.

- origin (how did it start?): formed spontaneously from students aged 16 to 18 years who met each other because they were in the same year group at school. Several members got to know each other to start with, and others have joined the group since.
- leadership (how is it led?): there is no formal leader, although one or two members usually have a dominant role and suggest group activities. The identity of these members tends to change over time, however.
- size (how many members?): there are currently about eight members of this group, although there is no fixed minimum or maximum.
- members (who can be a member?): no formal criteria for membership exist, although new members tend to be accepted by consensus (informal agreement) of other group members
- outcome (what is its purpose?): to allow group members to interact socially with one another, most often informally.
- programme (what activities does it undertake?): there is not always a defined activity for the group, although sometimes group members might plan to go to a cafe together, go into town for the evening or share lunch and break times together at school. Activities are usually chosen to facilitate the group outcome of social interaction.

Group 2: A Level class in a school

- origin (how did it start?): the group was formally created at the start of the academic year by school administrators as part of the school's student enrolment and timetabling arrangements.
- leadership (how is it led?): a teacher, assigned to the class by the school, and significantly older than the other members (who are all 16 or 17 years old) has a formally recognised leadership role and directs the activities of the group.
- size (how many members?): there are 20 student members of the group and one teacher.
- members (who can be a member?): the leader must be a member of the school's academic staff in the relevant subject department and is allocated by the school's administrators. The students are also allocated to the group administratively. They must be students in the school in the relevant year group, and for most courses they will have elected to be members by choosing that A Level as part of their academic programme. In order to do this, they must also qualify for membership because of their previous academic achievements.
- outcome (what is its purpose?): the formally defined purpose of the group is for its student members to complete the programme of learning associated with the A Level and gain it as a qualification by passing the required examinations.
- programme (what activities does it undertake?): group members meet at agreed times in a classroom at the school to undertake learning activities set by the group leader which will help them to achieve the group outcome.

Collaboration

Group 3: Saturday customer retail team in a clothing store

- origin (how did it start?): the retail team was established by the regional management of the company who own the retail company in order to set up a store in that location. They did this by advertising for members and choosing them through a selection process for employment.

- leadership (how is it led?): this customer retail team is led by a shift supervisor who has also been recruited and allocated to the group.

- size (how many members?): there are four sales assistants plus the shift supervisor.

- members (who can be a member?): only those individuals recruited by store management and allocated to each role can be members.

- outcome (what is its purpose?): the purpose of the group is to generate profit for the retail company by assisting customers with their purchasing decisions and selling items of clothing to them.

- programme (what activities does it undertake?): the group approaches customers to discuss purchasing decisions, completes sales transactions, processes clothing stock and organises store displays in order to serve the overall group purpose.

As you can see from these three examples, the nature of groups can vary dramatically depending on the different criteria which make them up. What we can also see is that whether a group is successful or not, and how we measure that success, is closely linked to how it is established, what it is supposed to do and what it is supposed to achieve. Knowing these criteria for the group you are part of is therefore extremely important.

ACTIVITY 6.02

Choose a group you are part of – it could be a personal friendship group, or one you are in at school or work. Using Douglas's headings, describe the group as in each of the three examples above.

Measuring group success and failure

A group is successful if it is achieving, or has achieved, its intended outcome. Successful activities, therefore, are those which are bringing about that outcome, and the most effective group members are those who also work to achieve those goals.

We can measure group failure in the same way. Groups that are not successful in achieving their intended outcome usually find themselves in this position either because their activities are not organised in a way that will bring about their intended outcome, or because group members do not act in appropriate ways with each other.

ACTIVITY 6.03

Choose one of the groups you are familiar with which you listed in Activity 6.01. If this group was to fail in its intended outcome, what would be the cause of this? It might help to imagine yourself as part of this group: what are the things that could go wrong, and how would they make it an unsuccessful group experience?

Divide the causes of group failure into two categories:

- causes that are due to the activities of the group
- causes that are due to the members of the group.

Reflection: You will hopefully have come up with a range of causes which are appropriate to the situation of your chosen group. As an example, if we take Group 3 in the reflection point in Activity 6.01 (the sales team in a clothing store), here are some of the points you might have made for comparison:

Failures of group activities	Failures of group members
Incorrect or insufficient supplies of clothing are ordered.	Team leader does not listen to ideas of staff.
Displays are incomplete or organised in confusing ways so items cannot be easily located.	Team members do not attend work consistently.
Customers are ignored or treated rudely.	Staff argue over who is to perform which role.
Customers feel overwhelmed, as they are approached by too many staff at once.	One person is excessively dominant and upsets or intimidates staff or customers.
No one is available to process transactions.	
Pricing is incorrectly applied to items (including sales discounts).	

Evaluating group roles

In order to consider the success or failure of the group's activities, and especially of its members, it is necessary to consider the role each plays in more detail. A number of different ideas have been suggested about this, and there are several theories of group roles which categorise what each member of a group does in different ways.

One set of categories which might be helpful was proposed by Kurt Albrecht. This places group members into one of five roles depending on what they do in the group:

Task roles

- Ideas people: think about what needs to be done
- Action people: ensure that what has been decided upon gets done

Group roles

- Organisers: make sure things are done efficiently
- Energisers: provide motivation to the group
- Uncommitted: make no real contribution

These categories also recognise the importance of both managing the tasks or activities of the group and the group members in their relationships. They also recognise that if a group is not functioning well, it is often due to the fact that one or more group members are uncommitted, and are not making a contribution at any given time.

ACTIVITY 6.04

Think about your own role when you have been involved in group activities in the past. Have you focused on the task, or the group, or have you tended to be uncommitted? Would you regard yourself as an ideas or action person, or an organiser or energiser?

You should also consider the following:

- Have you played different roles at different stages of a group task, or played more than one role?
- Have you played different roles depending on the group? Is this based on what you were doing, or who you were working with?
- Are Albrecht's roles helpful, or would different categories best describe what you have done in groups?

If you are discussing this task with others, you could also ask them whether they think you play these roles, and also give your opinion on what they do when they are with you.

Reflection: There is no right answer to this activity, and you may come up with a variety of different responses. You may not have considered your function within a group before, or you might have a very clear idea about the role you play. It is important to also bear in mind that roles are not necessarily fixed: it is possible to focus more on the task or the group members, and to do different things within these areas, depending on the context of what you are doing. You may even have decided that these categories do not properly describe what you do in a group situation.

Another point to consider is that how you think you are behaving in a group, and how others see you as behaving, is not the same thing as what you are actually doing in each situation. You might feel that you are making an effective contribution to the group's purpose, or that you are performing a specific function, but others in the group may not see it in that way. This is why it can be very important to discuss the effectiveness of a group with other people who have also been part of it, and get their views in order to have a fully rounded picture.

The most common cause of group failure is when individuals simply do not contribute to the group's overall purpose, or do not participate in its activities. Identifying when this is happening is therefore an important part of evaluating group work, or weighing up and judging whether or not it is effective in fulfilling the purposes of the group. But even for those group members who are making a contribution, knowing what their intended role is, and whether others also see it in that way offers important information to help us decide if the group is working well.

There are a number of other outlines of group roles apart from Albrecht's. One is R.M. Belbin's team roles theory, which suggests nine possible functions for members of a group: resource investigator, team-worker, co-ordinator, plant, monitor evaluator, specialist, shaper, implementer, completer-finisher. You can find out more about them, and what they mean, by going to http://www.belbin.com/about/belbin-team-roles/.

After doing this, you may want to assess how useful these categories are, or to look into whether you can find out about any more ideas about the roles people play in groups, or how groups work successfully.

Group theory and practice

In looking at how people work in groups, we have been looking at some ideas which explain in general how people in groups tend to behave. These general ideas, known as **theories**, can be helpful in showing us what to look for in group interactions we might have, and also in allowing us to test out our experiences of how working in groups happens in **practice**: in other words, what happens when we actually get involved in activities with groups of people. Having a set of expectations also allows us to make judgements about how we perform in group work, and how successful our groups are in accomplishing their purpose.

Discussion point

How helpful have you been finding these theories in explaining what happens in practice with groups in your own life? Are there any occasions where what is expected in theory differs from what happens in practice, and can you explain this?

Being able to evaluate how we work in groups is an important skill, as it allows us to make judgements about our effectiveness and to improve our performance in the future, as well as being able to account for why we work in groups in the way we do. Having knowledge of theories about group work, and the theorists, or experts, who have developed them is not important in itself. You might choose to use them, or other theories, or your own ideas, but it is most important to be able to make judgements about your work in groups, give reasons for those judgements and use this to improve the way you work with other people in the future.

6.02 Introducing the team project

It is important to understand that the team project is a specific group work task with its own requirements and activities. The Cambridge International AS & A Level Global Perspectives & Research syllabus describes that task as the following sequence of steps:

1 Form a group of two or five people with the assistance of your teacher.
2 Work together to identify a problem which is local to you as a group, but also has global relevance.
3 Allocate each group member to a different aspect of the problem so they can use this to propose their own solution from that perspective.
4 Have individual group members give presentations of up to eight minutes to an audience to propose their own solution and demonstrate why they consider it to be better than the others available.

5 Following this, have group members come together to agree a set of solutions to the problem.

6 Finally, have each group member write an 800-word paper reflecting on their experience undertaking the task.

Stages 4 and 6 will be dealt with in Chapters 7 and 8, as these relate to the individual assessments which will allow you to show what you have achieved from the team experience, and are not group tasks at all.

Steps 1–5, however, could be rewritten as a group description using Douglas's criteria which were introduced in Section 6.01:

- origin (how did it start?): created by the teacher of a Global Perspectives & Research class for the purpose of completing the team project component of the qualification
- leadership (how is it led?): supported in its initial stages by a teacher who is outside the group; the group itself may or may not decide to select a leader formally, although members playing leadership roles may informally emerge.
- size (how many members?): there must be a minimum of two and a maximum of five members, although sizes within this range are also acceptable.
- members (who can be a member?): students doing AS or A Level Global Perspectives & Research who wish to complete the requirements of the team project must be included in the membership of a team project group.
- outcome (what is its purpose?): to define a local problem with global relevance and to propose a range of individual solutions to this problem drawing on contrasting perspectives, as well as an overall group solution. The solutions must be effective and workable.
- programme (what activities does it undertake?): decide on a local problem which is suitable for the group to work on, produce research on this problem, use the research to allocate separate perspectives on the problem to group members, agree on a group solution which draws on individual solutions each member has developed using their selected perspective.

Discussion point

Does your team project group at your school follow this description? Talk about this with the other members of your group. If it does not, discuss what changes might be required.

The decisions you make as a group and the success you achieve will be in relation to these criteria, so it will be important for you to bear these in mind.

ACTIVITY 6.05

Given what you now know about the outcome and programme of the team project, what do you think are the specific routines and activities which would be most useful to achieve this?

Also think about what the members of the team should do. Using a theory of group roles, think about the most useful roles for this group and how group members should work together.

KEY TERMS

agenda: a list of the items to be covered in a meeting which is produced in advance. It also usually includes the time and location of the meeting and who will be attending.

minutes: a written record of what is discussed in a meeting under each of the agenda points and any agreed points for action after the meeting, with who is to do each and by when. One of the people attending the meeting is usually given the task of producing the minutes.

Reflection: There is no right answer to this activity, because your plans for how your group will work to achieve the team's outcomes will depend on your own circumstances. You may, however, have considered some of the following:

- Will you organise meetings for major decisions, such as deciding on your team's chosen problem, allocating perspectives to each team member, and reviewing an overall team solution?

- Will there be regular ways of keeping in touch between these major meetings? Will these also involve getting together face to face, or would you also make use of mobile telephones or social media?

- How will you record and share notes on the information which has been researched by the group as a whole, before individuals work on their own perspectives and presentations?

- Will anyone be responsible for calling and co-ordinating meetings, for deciding on a schedule for what is to be discussed (called an **agenda**) and taking notes of what has been said (called **minutes**).

- Do you think you should decide formally on any of the roles such as those focused on generating tasks and ensuring they are done, or organising the group? Which roles, if any, will you allow to emerge spontaneously as the group works together?

- How important is it that there are people to motivate the group? How should they go about doing this?

As with the other activities in this chapter which have invited you to think about how groups work together, it might be helpful for you to get the views of other students you know. They may share your views or have different feelings about this.

6.03 Selecting suitable problems and identifying solutions

In the previous section we summarised the required outcome for each team project group as follows:

> To define a local problem with global relevance and to propose a range of individual solutions to this problem drawing on contrasting perspectives, as well as an overall group solution. The solutions must be effective and workable.

The requirement for your group's problem to be 'local with global relevance', which is taken from the syllabus, is deliberately lacking in detail because it is designed to allow you and your fellow students to investigate a problem which is genuinely meaningful to your own local situation, wherever you are in the world, as well as having a potentially global relevance. It will also be a problem for which it will be worthwhile to find solutions, and for which those solutions would make a meaningful difference in the world.

This section therefore gives you some guidance about how you can formulate your problem, and some case studies of how other students in different schools all over the world have identified suitable problems for them to investigate and propose solutions.

Stating a problem

In Chapter 4 (in Section 4.03), we outlined three different kinds of question –imperatives, interrogatives and declaratives – which are appropriate for three different kinds of task. We saw that the first, imperatives or commands, are often used in written examinations (like Component 1), where we are instructed to find something specific in a text, or carry out a particular analytical or evaluative task using the skills of deconstruction. In Component 2, the essay, on the other hand, interrogatives are more useful as they invite us to explore alternatives in a specific issue before coming to a judgement, such as 'Should religious organisations be involved in education?' or 'Is the removal of barriers to international trade a good thing?'.

In Component 3, however, your team is being asked to state a potential problem, so a statement, or declarative, is the best kind of phrase to use to do this. Here are some examples:

- Access to clean drinking water
- Rising sea levels
- Prices of pharmaceuticals
- Lack of access to the internet.

Each of these statements describes a problem which needs to be solved, both in a specific local area and in other places across the globe. They also act as prompts for the group to do the following:

- explain what the problem is
- use research to provide evidence that it is a problem
- ensure that this research gives examples of the problem in the group's own locality and in other areas in the world to show that it has global relevance.

The case studies that follow explain how different groups have set about doing these things with their problem statements.

Case Study 1: Income inequality

Income inequality is the gap between those who have the highest financial incomes in a location and those who have the lowest. One team started with the syllabus topic of Global Economic Activity and identified that, over time, there has been a growing gap between the income levels of the wealthiest, most developed countries of the world and the least developed. The wealthiest 8.1% of the global population hold 84.6% of global wealth.

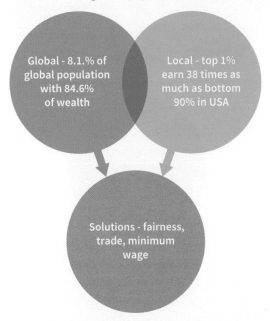

At the same time, however, in many Western countries, there has also been a growing gap between the richest and poorest within the country. The group discovered that this gap was largest within their own country, the United States, where it has been growing significantly over the last few decades. Americans in the top 1% of income now earn 38 times as much as those in the bottom 90%. In the group's own local community in Florida, they discovered that this income inequality was the fifth highest in the country, demonstrating that the problem is of sharp local as well as global significance.

Having conducted research to establish evidence for the scope of the problem both locally and globally, it was then the task of group members to identify separate solutions. They did this by identifying a number of different approaches to the problem which could be organised under the themes of Global Perspectives & Research, which we introduced in Chapter 3. One group member saw this as an ethical problem, and researched ideas for restoring fairness to income distribution by measuring it against a moral standard. Another group member saw income inequality as a purely economic issue, which could be solved by wealth creation through trade. Finally, a third member focused on political assumptions and researched solutions which rely on public policy, such as a minimum wage and taxation measures focused on the wealthy.

Case study 2: Refugee quotas

Globally, refugees are people who are forced to leave the country where they live because of war, persecution or natural disaster. The 1951 Refugee Convention, an international agreement, states that refugees should not be returned to a country where they face serious threats to their life and freedom. Although the convention states that all countries are required to consider the applications of all refugees who arrive within their borders, many countries also participate in an arrangement with the United Nations on the permanent resettlement of refugees so that they have a specific annual quota, or number, of accepted refugees whom they will allow to settle in their country.

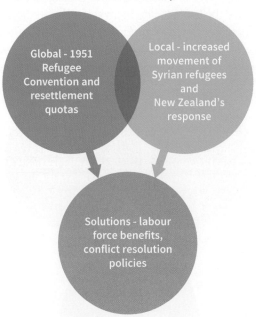

A team of two students at a school in New Zealand identified that this global issue, relevant to the syllabus topic of both Migration and Work and Ethical Foreign Policies, was also of local significance in their own country. This is because the government of New Zealand has recognised that the conflict within Syria has generated an unusually high number of refugees globally. Their preferred solution to this problem is to increase New Zealand's agreed annual quota from 750 to 1,350 per year, with the additional 600 being made up of refugees from Syria.

Collaboration

Here the team was able to research the problem in its legal and political background. They also found that this was a situation where a solution had already been proposed by their country's government. One team member therefore decided to undertake further research to justify that solution. In doing this they drew on both ethical and economic themes, arguing that it was ethically correct to accept additional refugees if they were in need, and economically that settling additional refugees into New Zealand would produce economic benefits by adding them to the labour force. The other team member argued that the solution was not to increase refugee quotas in smaller countries like New Zealand, but instead to rely on larger countries taking them in and also to develop policies to address the causes of the conflict in Syria. This drew on political and cultural themes, claiming that the presence of additional Syrian refugees posed a security risk to New Zealand, and that they would find it difficult to integrate into New Zealand because of language barriers and the need to adjust to a different way of life.

Case study 3: Education and employment

The potential social and economic benefits of education are recognised by many countries globally. This is shown by the significant proportion of national income which is spent on education, especially in industrialised countries, and the close attention paid by governments to benchmarks of educational standards, such as the PISA rankings published by the OECD. The evidence for the employment benefits of tertiary education (in other words, education beyond secondary-level, or third-stage education) is particularly strong. Statistics show that in European Union countries the employment rate for tertiary graduates is 78.3% whereas it is only 58.9% for non-tertiary graduates.

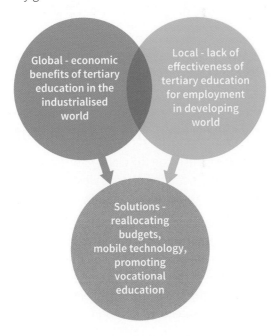

The global situation therefore seems to suggest that education is a solution, not a problem. However, the team of three students at a school in Zimbabwe observed that the relationship between investment in education and employment outcomes does not hold as well in developing countries. The evidence shows that, in Zimbabwe for example, the majority of people educated to tertiary level are unemployed.

A variety of explanations exist for this disparity, and within the team each member focused on economic, technological and political perspectives respectively when diagnosing the situation and arguing for solutions. These produced solutions which ranged from reallocating budgets so that money within the educational system is more efficiently spent on generating better outcomes, to introducing mobile technology to provide education in more flexible ways which better prepare students for employment and changing education policy so that vocational training, linked to specific skills and professions, is offered as a viable alternative to more general, academic routes.

ACTIVITY 6.06

Look at the text and diagrams for each of the case studies. What do they have in common in terms of the stages each group went through?

What do you notice about:

- how each team supported their work on the problems they selected with evidence
- the relationship between the global and local situations
- the differences between each of the solutions which are proposed?

Section 6.04, on the role of the Critical Path in supporting the team project, should help you to reflect on your answers to this activity.

Discussion point

Having read the examples in these case studies, get together with several other students and mind-map at least four problems in your local area (town, city, region or your part of the world) which also have global significance and you can link to at least one of the topics in the Cambridge International AS & A Level Global Perspectives & Research syllabus.

If you can, then take one of them and mind-map at least two alternative perspectives on the problem.

It does not matter whether you discuss this with students who are members of your team project group or not: the idea here is to test out possible problems that are relevant to your locality.

6.04 The team project and the Critical Path

This chapter has been very much focused on the element of collaboration within the Critical Path, and rightly so, as the team project is the place in which you are called on to develop your collaborative skills in a group in order to successfully carry out the required tasks.

Collaboration, however, is only one stage of the Critical Path, and, along with communication, works to support and inform the other stages of deconstruction, reconstruction and reflection. In the team project you are asked to reflect on the solutions you develop and the judgements on the team problem they involve. In fact, as we have also seen, there is an opportunity to record this reflection in the 800-word reflective paper, and so reflection is dealt with in much more detail in Chapter 8, which addresses this part of the task.

This leaves deconstruction and reconstruction and the relationship between them, which should still drive your research as part of the team project as well as your presentation of its results. You may have noticed that each of the teams in the previous section's case studies supported their identification of the problem with evidence. This evidence justified the existence of the problem in a local and a global context. It was also always the strongest and most secure evidence for the problem, drawn from a variety of different sources. In this sense, the team was already having to make evaluative judgements in establishing the situation, and they were also combining and comparing claims and evidence in a way that added the skills of reconstruction to deconstruction.

Collaboration

Finally, and most importantly, in developing your own solutions from the team's research, you are making arguments, which is central to the process of the Critical Path. These are located in a specific perspective, which is made up of reasoning, evidence and a set of assumptions from a particular context. Each of the teams in the case studies used Global Perspectives & Research themes (e.g. economics, politics, culture) as a starting point for these, and that may well be sensible as it makes it easier to ensure that each group member has a contrasting perspective and all group members are clear about what everyone is doing. However, this theme is only the beginning. It will support a range of collected items of evidence which support one another, and a range of arguments from linked sources which share common assumptions in order to close down any inferential gaps.

It is also important to be aware that at the end of the process the group will come back together to agree a group solution. By its nature, this cannot be one which incorporates all the elements of the various, contrasting individual solutions. However, by still applying the Critical Path, it will be possible to break down their elements, and combine evidence, or assumptions, or reasoning or contexts wherever necessary in order to construct solutions with the widest possible range of agreement.

It is also important to bear in mind that the only elements of the team project which are directly assessed are the eight-minute presentation and 800-word reflective paper, so each of the two following chapters is concerned with demonstrating the skills of the Critical Path actively in these.

ACTIVITY 6.07

Re-read Chapters 2 and 3 of this book, focusing on the skills of deconstruction and reconstruction involved in evaluating individual sources and combining them into perspectives.

Make a list of three skills from these chapters you do well and can immediately apply to your work on the team project.

Make a list of three skills you feel less confident with and need to practise further before applying them in the team project.

These skills might include things like identifying arguments, evaluating evidence and the context of sources, defining perspectives and planning research.

Summary

In this chapter we have:

- assessed the benefits and challenges involved in working together with others
- described and evaluated a range of approaches to groups and group roles
- summarised the requirements of the team project
- explored how to work with members of your team to identify a local problem with global significance
- discussed a range of case studies for possible team project tasks
- linked the skills assessed by the team project to the Critical Path.

Although your collaboration with others is not assessed directly by either of the individual tasks you will need to complete for your team project, it is a skill which is essential to successfully identifying and carrying out the task you will then need to respond to in your presentation and comment on in your reflective paper. Beyond this, however, working with others is an important skill for life, and your work in this chapter should give you some tools for understanding and improving what happens when you find yourself in a group.

Practising collaboration for the team project

This section of the chapter is divided into three: firstly, establishing collaborative skills, secondly, developing collaborative skills and finally, enhancing collaborative skills. Each section is designed to build on the one before. You can either work through each section in turn or choose the section which you feel is at the most appropriate level for you. However, you will notice that some of the questions are linked, so you should attempt the question in a previous section before moving on to the connected question in the later section.

You should also see a progression of difficulty through the three levels, but they are also aligned in this chapter to the distinctive skills we have established.

These sections use a variety of topics from the Cambridge International AS & A Level Global Perspectives & Research syllabus. Some are specified, but in other cases you are invited to choose your own. This is intended to be part of your continued progression towards working on your own initiative as you collaborate as part of a group on the team project.

Establishing collaborative skills

Consider what you have learnt about working in groups from following the course so far, before starting work on the team project. This might include the group presentation activity in Chapter 1, as well as other group discussion tasks you might have participated in. Make notes on the following points:

- What has been positive about these group work experiences?
- What has been challenging?
- How do you think the group work might have developed you as a student of Global Perspectives & Research?

When you have made your notes, share them with one or two other people who are following the course and compare what they have written.

Finally, feed back as a group to the rest of your class, or another group of students, summarising the similarities and differences in your experiences and what the value of undertaking this activity has been.

Developing collaborative skills

1   If you undertook the task in the previous section, you could also consider what roles you have tended to play in the previous group activities on the course and in that group activity. Do they fit into Albrecht's categories, or another set you have researched, such as Belbin's? What ideas do you have about the role you tend to play when you work with others and the impact it makes?

2   When you have done this, share your thoughts with one or two other students and listen to their views on group roles. If you can, it might be good to do this task with students who are not part of your group for the team project so you can get a different perspective.

3   Meet with a group of two to five students to review how the Global Perspectives & Research course has gone so far. Select one person to gather ideas for an agenda (the order of points you will discuss). They will also chair the meeting, which means they are responsible for starting and finishing it, and ensuring that the meeting moves through the points on the agenda in order and in good time so that the meeting lasts the agreed duration. Someone else should also be responsible for taking minutes of what is discussed and recording any action points for people to do after the meeting.

In order to help you with this task, suggested templates for writing an agenda and recording minutes are given below. You should feel free, however, to research or design your own as long as your versions cover the essential functions of an agenda and minutes.

Template for a formal agenda

Meeting Agenda

Date, time and location of meeting:

Type of meeting:

Name of meeting chair:

1   Note of who is present and any apologies sent for those being absent
2   Review of minutes of any previous meeting held to check action points
3   Issues for discussion (these are numbered from this point)
4   Agreement on date and location for next meeting

Template for formal minutes

Meeting Minutes

Date, time and location of meeting:

Type of meeting:

Name of meeting chair:

1   List of group members present and any group members who apologised for being absent
2   Confirmation that minutes from last meeting were checked and approved
3   Short summary of what was discussed under each point on the agenda and list of agreed actions with who is to do them (these are numbered from this point)
4   Summary list of actions, people to do actions, and dates actions to be done by
5   Statement of agreed date and location for next meeting

Enhancing collaborative skills

In the group of two to five students you have been allocated for the team project, meet to decide on the problem you will select. Your teacher will support you in doing this. Ensure you make use of an agenda and minutes.

As the case studies suggested, you may like first to select a topic from the syllabus and discuss why an issue from it is globally relevant before exploring how it might show itself in your local area.

When you have done this, allocate tasks to research the problem and gather a variety of evidence about it.

The final stage of the task is to meet again to discuss your research findings and decide on different aspects for each team member to develop into a separate perspective and their own solution.

Chapter 7
Communication: team project presentations

Learning aims

By the end of this chapter, you should be able to:

- outline the features of effective presentations
- show how an effective oral presentation differs from an essay
- prepare effectively for giving your presentation
- make an effective argument using your presentation
- use visual aids to support your presentation
- produce an engaging and convincing personal performance.

This chapter will support you with giving individual presentations as part of team projects. Chapters 6, 7 and 8 cover the different aspects of the team project.

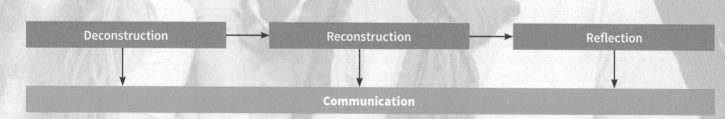

| Deconstruction | → | Reconstruction | → | Reflection |

| Communication |

Introduction

Team projects require a combination of collaborative and individual work to produce a successful outcome. As we saw in Chapter 6, you need to work well in a group to select and research a suitable problem, and to come together at the end to agree on a group solution. However, alongside this you need to produce two pieces of *individual* work on which you will be assessed. These are an individual oral presentation, of eight minutes, which we will look at in this chapter, and an 800-word paper reflecting on your experiences of undertaking your team project (which is discussed in Chapter 8).

In the oral presentation, you will do several different things:

- explain and provide evidence for the global and local significance of your team's chosen problem
- show how your perspective on the problem differs from those of the others in your team, and why you consider your approach to be the best one
- argue for your chosen solutions, providing reasons and evidence for why they are effective and innovative
- do these things in a way that engages and convinces your audience, using techniques appropriate for an oral presentation.

These requirements draw on several linked elements of the Critical Path, but they are all joined by your ability to communicate. When you organise evidence and provide reasons leading to conclusions, you will be drawing on the skills of deconstruction and reconstruction. However, they will be served by your ability to present your work as an effective communication to an audience.

This chapter therefore aims to show how communication works with each aspect of the individual presentation in order to produce a successful outcome.

ACTIVITY 7.01

Can you recall an effective presentation you have seen, either in school or somewhere else? Think about what made the speaker effective:

- Was it the way in which they made the material they were presenting interesting?
- Was it the clarity of their message?

If you wish, you may choose to explore some of the talks on the TED website (www.ted.com), especially those in the playlist of the 20 most shared talks. TED is a charitable organisation dedicated to spreading ideas in the form of 'short, powerful talks' of up to 18 minutes. Find a talk on this site which you feel is effective and answer these questions about it.

Reflection: Here are some of the factors that may make a presentation effective for an audience. You may have mentioned some of the following and recalled examples of them in your chosen presentation:

- the subject of the presentation
- the performance of the presenter through gesture and tone of voice
- personal information used to make the presentation more engaging
- a range of visual aids (not necessarily just PowerPoint slides)

- appropriate level of language for the audience
- clear and logical connections between each point that is made.

Perhaps the most relevant aspect of an oral presentation is its memorability: what makes you recall its details, and what about it sticks in your mind. Achieving this when you are only standing in front of your audience for a maximum of eight minutes is one of the most challenging, but also rewarding, aspects of giving the presentation.

7.01 Audience and purpose

The starting point for any kind of presentation, or communication of any sort, is to consider its **audience** and **purpose**. In other words, who it is for and what it is trying to achieve?

If we compare these two aspects of the presentation and the essay, there are some interesting differences, as well as similarities, between them.

The audiences for your essay and your presentation are quite different:

- The essay will be read at a computer screen by an individual, who may move up and down through the document to review and re-read it at their own pace. That individual will almost certainly read the essay at a different time to that at which it was written and in a different place. The writer of the essay need not be present when it is read.
- The presentation will be heard by, potentially, a group of people. It will be delivered by the presenter in their presence and there will be no opportunity to pause or repeat the performance. The audience will experience it continuously and once only.

There are some similarities and differences in the purpose of the essay and presentation.

Similarities:

- Both the essay and the presentation have the purpose of making an argument: supporting a conclusion with reasons.
- Both the essay and the presentation aim to answer a question (although in the case of the presentation it is formulated as a problem statement).

Differences:

- The purpose of the essay is to analyse and evaluate at least two perspectives arising from the question before coming to a judgement in the conclusion.
- The purpose of the presentation is to explain the team problem before arguing for a solution from the presenter's chosen perspective.

The difference in purpose between the essay and the presentation can be summarised as to say that the presentation is more *persuasive* than the essay. Your main purpose is to show your chosen perspective and that the solutions which are based on it are stronger and more convincing than the alternatives which are available.

Communication

Discussion point
Given how the audience and purpose of the presentation compare to those of the essay, how would you go about preparing and delivering it?

7.02 Preparing for your presentation

Giving an effective oral presentation is all about preparation and planning. You need to know as much as possible in advance about how you will be delivering your presentation and what will be required for you to be ready. Here are some good questions to start with:

- Where and when will the presentation take place?
- How big will your audience be, and who will be in it? This will partly depend on the capacity of the room and the timing of when the presentation takes place.
- How well lit is the room, and is there the capacity to make it dark if required?
- What computer equipment will be available to you? This may include the operating system (e.g. Windows or Mac), presentation software (PowerPoint or something else), internet connection, a projector and screen and the ability to play sound if required.
- How will you arrange recording your presentation using a video camera? This is required as part of the Global Perspectives & Research assessment.
- Is it likely that you will be able to give your presentation without interruptions, either from people coming into the room, or from sounds from elsewhere in the building which might disturb your presentation or its recording?

Knowing how your presentation will be assessed before you start working on it is very useful. Your teacher will almost certainly be sitting in the room to support you along with your audience, but they will not be formally assessing your work. Instead, it will be video recorded and sent electronically to be marked while being watched on a computer screen.

Your teacher will have some technical instructions for the required file size and format, and how to transmit the files. However, this does mean that it is important the recording be as clear as possible, so your performance can be properly seen and heard. It also means that the eight minute limit for the length of the presentation is very important, as the person marking it will stop the video recording at that point and not watch any more.

You will be required to submit a transcript of the presentation – an exact written record of what you say – but as we will explain later, it is best that you do not produce this until the end of the process. What is useful at the beginning, as a guide, is to know how many words you will be able to speak in eight minutes. On average, at a measured pace (which is important to make it effective), people can speak between 110 and 120 words per minute. This means that you will be able to say between 880 and 960 words in total in your presentation, and this is a good range to plan around. As we will also see later, some rehearsal – and recording yourself – will be very useful, as this will help you to work out what you can comfortably deliver.

In a presentation, however, your words are not all that matters. Much of the success of your delivery will also depend on the visual aids you use to support and illustrate what you say. More detailed advice on this will be given later in the chapter, but it is certainly worth considering your options at this early stage. Many people will automatically opt for software which displays slides of information on a large display or projector, such as Microsoft's PowerPoint or Apple's Keynote. However, there are a number of other options you may not have considered. For example:

- Prezi (https://www.prezi.com): a non-linear presentation format which allows you to plot a path through a canvas of text and images
- Haiku Deck (https://www.haikudeck.com): presentation slides which build many of the design elements of effective presentations into the system itself
- a non-digital presentation system, such as a poster you have created on the wall behind you, or pre-prepared sheets of flipchart paper
- objects you can show to illustrate points you make.

ACTIVITY 7.02

Use one of the methods listed above to produce a short (five-minute) presentation on a hobby or other personal interest. Aim to choose a method you have not had any experience of trying previously.

Reflection: How did you find the process of learning and using a different method of presentation? Make a list of reasons why each of these methods may be more or less effective than using software based on electronic slides, such as Microsoft PowerPoint.

(You may also have considered finding or making video clips and showing them as part of your presentation. These can be effective sometimes, but you should be cautious with showing them, as they will reduce the amount of time you have to speak and make your case within the eight minutes you have available.)

ACTIVITY 7.03

Find out the practical details of:
- where and when you will be presenting
- who will be in your audience
- arrangements for recording your presentation.

Also give some thought to how possible interruptions will be prevented, and what methods you might consider to support your presentation visually.

Discussion point

Discussing the practical details with other members of your team or class will also be useful.

Rehearsing for your performance

Your final presentation will be a performance, not unlike the performance of an actor on the stage. For this reason, it is very important that a major part of your preparation involves rehearsal.

Communication

Rehearsing for your performance means practising parts of it, or the whole presentation, in order to test that it will work successfully with the resources you have in the time available. To do this, you should ideally practise with the same visual aids as you will be using for your final presentation, and also use a timer to ensure that you present within the allowed eight minutes. Focused rehearsal will also help you to develop your verbal fluency and level of skill in presenting your material.

Start by giving some of your presentation to an audience. At first, this audience might just be a mirror – sometimes family pets are useful if you want something to focus on! A really important requirement for improving your level of skill, however, is to get feedback on what you have done. Here, you may present to a friend, family member or perhaps the other members of your team. Those other members of your team may well be your most effective audience, as they may be able to evaluate your performance, judging how well you have responded to the advice given in this chapter, or your teacher making suggestions for improvements.

Discussion point

Talk about your performance to someone else who has seen you rehearse. Ask them what they found more or less effective about your performance and consider what you would keep the same or change as a result. Make sure you compare the suggestions you get to feedback from others and sources of advice, such as that in this book.

As you rehearse, you will also need to give some consideration to the prompts you will use to ensure you make your intended points in the right order and express them in the best way. Typing out the entire text of your presentation in advance and reading it from a sheet or computer screen might seem to be safest, but this means that it will be difficult to keep eye contact with your audience and to ensure that they are fully engaged. On the other hand, speaking *extempore*, meaning without any written prompts at all, may be too much of a risk unless as part of your rehearsal you have memorised most or all of what you wish to say.

One useful compromise, employed by many presenters, is to have a collection of cue cards. These are usually index cards, obtained from stationery suppliers, where you write out the key points that you wish to say. They can then be numbered or colour-coded so you use them in the right order, and you can glance down at each as a starting point to be expanded on without becoming disengaged from your audience.

7.03 Structuring your presentation

In following the course so far, we have recognised the importance of effectively structuring arguments, whether they are in the form of articles you encounter in your research, or essays you write. The structure of your presentation is equally important. However, it also shows a number of distinctive features of its own because of its audience and purpose.

The three parts of a presentation

In Chapter 5 we saw the importance of using signposts in essays. These show the reader where they are in the essay, what has been covered and what is coming next. Signposts are even more important in presentations. This is because you are speaking to an audience who will not have the opportunity to read or review what you say.

The starting point for effectively signposting your presentation is to divide it into three parts: an introduction, main body and conclusion. In this, the presentation has the same structure as the essay. Each of these three parts, however, has a different purpose.

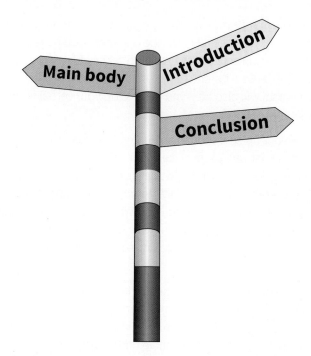

The introduction

In the introduction to your presentation you will need to introduce yourself and the topic of your presentation. You need to let your audience know who you are, what you are speaking about and why this is significant.

The introduction also lists the areas you will cover in the main body of your presentation. This will help your audience as they will know what to expect from what you are going to say, and how each part of your argument will fit together.

The main body

The main body of a presentation takes up nearly all of its length and contains all of its important content. It is here that you will set out the evidence for your team's problem, show how your perspective differs from those of others in your team, and argue for your solutions. You will do these things in the order you set out in your introduction, referring back to this at each stage.

The next section gives some examples of effective parts of the main body which achieve the objectives of the presentation.

The conclusion

Compared to the essay, the conclusion of the presentation is quite short. Its purpose is to summarise the content of the presentation you have just delivered and the order of topics you set out in your introduction. It allows your audience to be very clear on your key points and your main recommendations as the presentation concludes. In proposing realistic and workable solutions you are issuing a call to action to your audience that something should be done, and the conclusion is the best place to remind them what this is and to send them away from your presentation with this at the front of their minds.

(Sometimes at the end of a presentation there is also an opportunity to ask your audience if they have any questions and then to answer them, but this is not required for the team project presentation.)

Signposts within your argument

As well as the overall structure of your presentation, you can also create signposts in your argument itself, just as you do for the essay. These can include:

- Reason indicators: *first, second, third, finally, because*
- Conclusion indicators: *therefore, this means that, in conclusion*
- Changes of direction: *however, on the other hand, in contrast*
- Continuing in the same direction: *furthermore, in addition, also*

All of these signposts are exactly the same as those for the essay, and you should use them in your presentation in the same way. In fact, they are even more important in the presentation, as you need to ensure that the shape and direction of your argument are as clear as possible to your audience as they listen to you.

ACTIVITY 7.04

Prepare a presentation which makes an argument of your choice. This could be arguing that your school make a specific improvement, or an argument in support of another opinion you have. It should be about two minutes long.

However, you are not allowed to use any of the phrases for signposts within your argument listed above.

Give your presentation to someone else.

Reflection: Did you find not using any of the signpost phrases difficult? How did your audience respond to not having them? Why do you think this is?

7.04 Expressing your points in the main body

It is important to remember that you should not read your presentation from a complete script you have prepared in advance. This will make it hard for you to engage with your audience effectively. However, just as in the essay, the detail of how you construct each of your points, and the effectiveness of your argument, is very important. Because of this, 80% of the marks available in the presentation are for analysis and evaluation – the skills of deconstruction and reconstruction in the Critical Path – and the effectiveness of your communication is there to support that. What follows here are examples of effective practice for the various parts of the main body of your presentation.

Effectively differentiating your perspective

At some stage, ideally early in the main body of the presentation, you need to differentiate your perspective from those of the others in your team. As we saw in Chapter 6, part of the process of working with your team is to discuss and decide on different approaches to your problem so you can each develop your own contrasting solutions. When you come to write your reflective paper, you will also be analysing and evaluating this experience. However, this does not remove the need to explain for your audience what your perspective on the problem is and how this differs from other approaches, especially those of the other members of your team. If you do not do this in the presentation, then you cannot be rewarded for it.

What follows is an extract from a presentation on the availability of water which effectively states its own perspective and shows how it differs from that of other members of the team:

> One of my group members is looking at more efficient methods for storing and transporting water. Another one of my group members has suggested that central government could redistribute water to ensure that everyone gets some. And I am going to be describing ways in which we can use water less. By doing this I am going to be tackling the consumption, rather than the production or distribution of water, which sets me apart from my group members.

Not only does this presentation make clear their own approach and how it differs from the approaches of the others in their team, they also argue for why their approach is better, and so use this contrast to support their argument.

Effectively explaining the problem

It is also important that you spend some time in your presentation explaining the problem your group has chosen. This explanation will need to be supported by evidence so that you justify to your audience why this is a problem of local and global significance which needs to be solved. Doing this will make it easier to argue convincingly for your chosen solutions, and those arguments will have the advantage of being grounded firmly on the base of evidence you have set out at this stage of the presentation.

It is difficult to show an effective discussion of a problem without quoting from a presentation at length. If you do this effectively a significant proportion of your speaking time will be taken up with defining and evidencing your problem. However, there are a number of elements which you should aim to include:

- Clearly state what the issue is and why it is a problem.
- Give examples of why it is relevant in your local area and also in other parts of the world. There may be differences and similarities between these examples.
- Support your explanation of the problem with evidence. Ideally, you will use a variety of different kinds of evidence: for example, for a problem affecting the natural environment you may also include evidence of its economic and cultural impacts.

Remind yourself of the definition of an explanation from Chapter 3. For the purposes of the presentation, you are presenting the problem as a situation which you know to be true, and are providing reasons and evidence which explain it.

Effective and innovative solutions

Alongside your explanation of the problem and differentiation of your own perspective, the third main task of your presentation is to argue for your solution or solutions to the problem. This part of the presentation will be based on your research into solutions to your team's problem which come from your own perspective. However, you will also need to refer back to the evidence for the problem itself which you have already presented so you can show the links between the problem and the solution.

Your argument for your solution should be well developed: aim to devote at least half of the main body of your presentation to this after you have set out your own perspective and explained the problem. Aim to set out reasons and evidence which explain why your solution will be an **effective** answer to the problem. This means that you are attempting to demonstrate that it would have a measurable effect in the real world in solving the problem, or at least reducing its effects. Ideally, however, you should also show that your solution is **innovative**.

KEY TERMS

effective: having a measurable impact in changing a situation you have researched in a real-world situation

innovative: different to other solutions which have been used to deal with a problem

Communication

This means that it differs from solutions that have already been tried for the problem, and provides something which is new and better. You cannot, however, just assume that your audience will see that you have produced an innovative solution: you need to tell them this and show that you have considered other solutions and can identify why yours offers something different. Here is the end of the presentation quoted from earlier, which finishes its argument for its chosen solution by doing this:

> When my team and I sat down and tried to see which solution was better to deal with the problem of water supply, we found that no one solution was obviously better than the other. One person focused on the technologies of water, another person (myself) looked at the needs of consumers, and the third argued for political and economic solutions which could be implemented by governments. So, together we created a three-pronged solution to the problem of water. But, I alone, in proposing how communities can rethink the ways in which they use and share water, am challenging the assumption that the only solution to the problem of water is to supply more. Sometimes, the best solution to a difficulty is to rethink whether the problem really is what we think it is, and that is a genuinely fresh approach.

You are required to provide a transcript of your presentation along with the video recording of your performance. A transcript is not the same as a script because it is not produced before your presentation and you do not read from it. Instead, you should prepare your transcript by watching the video recording of your presentation and writing down what you say. When you do this you should not include any non-fluency features (sounds like 'umm' and 'err' and accidental repetition of words and phrases) but should record the exact words you use in the original order so that the person assessing your presentation can use the transcript to read along when watching the video of your performance.

7.05 Supporting your presentation with visuals

One of the most powerful features of your presentation is that you can use images and other visual elements to show your audience parts of your reasoning and evidence in ways that are more immediate, powerful and memorable than using words alone.

'Earthrise' was taken from *Apollo 8*, the first manned mission to the moon, on 24 December 1968. It was one of a series of pictures of the Earth from space which changed the way humans saw our planet and its place in the Universe.

A well-known English phrase is that 'a picture is worth a thousand words'. 'Earthrise' is one example of a picture which was effective in substituting for a large number of words or verbal discussion in changing the way we saw something, or giving a new insight. What other pictures can you think of from your own experience which have done something similar in making you see an issue afresh?

Slide design

Showing slides using a computer and projector is not the only way you can visually support your presentation. As we saw in Section 7.02, there are a number of other approaches you can use, including showing objects and preparing visual materials on posters or flipchart paper. However, the availability of slide presentation software and its appropriateness for many presentations means that it will still remain a popular option.

Despite the popularity of using slides, many presentations use them poorly. There are a number of reasons for this:

- Slides are used to display large amounts of text where a written document would be more appropriate.
- Bullet points are overused as prompts for the speaker, instead of supporting what they have to say.
- Pictures are often too small, and unclear in what they are intended to show.
- Other kinds of data, including graphs and charts, are over-complex and hard to interpret from the screen, or do not match well with the point the speaker wishes to make.

Often students are tempted to start with the slides, or even with the tools for creating the slides and the transitions between them, and then try to build a presentation which fits around them. Instead, you should begin with your ideas and arguments (which you will be delivering orally, not visually), then use slides carefully to support these in the best way.

When you are designing slides it is good to have these basic rules in mind:

- Work in units of three: three sections to the presentation, up to three linked slides to make a point, three bullet points per slide, up to three key words per bullet point. Less here is almost always more effective for your audience.
- Photographs can be more effective than clipart, so once you have a good photograph make it fill the whole slide so it speaks for itself. Speak about the photograph in your presentation and use it in your argument, rather than trying to explain it with additional text on the slide.
- Be consistent in your typography – use the same typeface and size of font for each type of heading, or bullet point, or key word. Introduce each new section with a header slide that works in the same way, so that your audience can identify your slide design as a set of signposts in itself.
- Ensure your text as well as your images can be seen. Anything less than 24 point text might be difficult to read from a distance, depending on the typeface used. It is always best to reduce the number of words on each slide and increase the number of slides used rather than reduce the size of the text.
- When it comes to making transitions between slides, less can be more, and it is often best to ignore over-complicated and distracting transitions in favour of clear and straightforward ones.

Slides filled with text are not effective

Slides filled with text are not effective. Slides filled with text are not effective. Slides filled with text are not effective. Slides filled with text are not effective. Slides filled with text are not effective. Slides filled with text are not effective. Slides filled with text are not effective. Slides filled with text are not effective. Slides filled with text are not effective. Slides filled with text are not effective. Slides filled with text are not effective. Slides filled with text are not effective. Slides filled with text are not effective. Slides filled with text are not effective. Slides filled with text are not effective. Slides filled with text are not effective. Slides filled with text are not effective.

Too many bullet points also don't work

- Bullet points may work well in written documents
- But they are rarely as successful on slides
- Too many bullet points give too much information for the audience
- Keep to a maximum of three per slide
- And think of other ways you can communicate the same information
- Otherwise you will end up with slides
- That look like this

Effective slide

'Earthrise' was taken from Apollo 8, the first manned mission to the moon, on 24 December 1968. It was one of a series of pictures of the Earth from space which changed the way humans saw our planet and its place in the Universe.

ACTIVITY 7.05

Make a slide that follows the advice given above for good slide design. You may base the content on a topic of your choice or something linked to a possible individual presentation for the team project.

Communication

Using real-world objects and other non-electronic resources

Using a physical object to help you make a point can have a very direct and powerful impact on your audience if used well. Objects can have two main purposes:

- to provide an example of the problem or solution you are illustrating. A loaf of bread, for instance, could be shown as part of a presentation about the relationship between farmers and the supply of food to supermarkets.

- to offer a metaphor for an argument you wish to make. For example, an apple could be cut into slices to show how resources are distributed in different proportions between contrasting groups of people.

If you do use objects, it is important to ensure that it is clear to your audience how the demonstration with the object supports your argument from what you say. You should also ensure that the object, and what you are doing with it, is clearly visible to everyone in the audience. In order to ensure this, you should consider the size of the object and how you will show it: you may lift it up, move it around or project it onto a large screen.

Other non-electronic resources can be used to display pictures, text or diagrams, either with posters or other printed or drawn documents. This method can be a good way for you to display skills or present evidence or ideas that cannot easily be captured by electronic formats. There is also the possibility, if you choose, of being able to develop your points visually in the presentation in real time, for example by writing points or drawing simple diagrams on sheets of flipchart paper.

If you do want to experiment with these methods, there are, however, some points for guidance you should consider:

- Many of the same design rules for electronic slides also apply to these: use a consistent approach and make sure that images and diagrams are linked to your argument and clearly understandable by your audience when they see them. You can do this by making sure that the key information is highlighted in an eye-catching and quickly digestible way.

- Think about how you will actually display the materials: is there an appropriate wall on which they will be mounted, or do you need some sort of stand? Are they the right size so the relevant details can be seen from 10, 20 or 30 feet away? The key is to consider your audience so that they see what you are intending them to see.

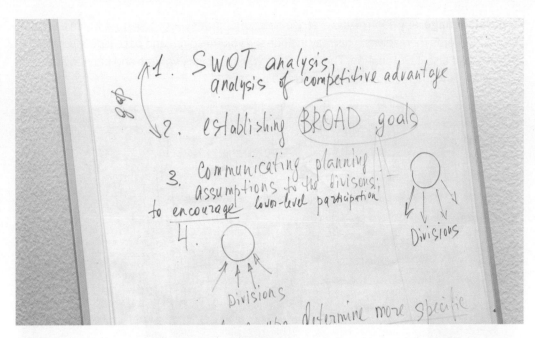

Presenting using a large poster is a commonly used approach, especially for giving presentations in universities. The following websites give some more detailed advice if you choose to adopt this approach:

- guide to how to create posters for academic presentations from New York University: **http://guides.nyu.edu/posters**

- poster presentation tips from Northern Arizona University, which also include advice on how to speak and deliver your presentation using a poster: **https://nau.edu/ undergraduate-research/poster-presentation-tips/**

- detailed study guide for producing poster presentations from the University of Leicester (UK) which outlines a number of alternative approaches: **https://nau.edu/ undergraduate-research/poster-presentation-tips/**.

7.06 Developing an effective personal performance

So far we have looked at two key aspects of your presentation: the words you will say in your argument and the visual aids you will use to support it. We have not yet addressed the third and, in some ways, most important element: yourself. The presentation is unique among the tasks you will undertake for assessment, as you will be present yourself in the video recording, rather than presenting your thoughts, ideas and arguments through the medium of writing. This means that how you present yourself and your personal performance are also something you will need to work on and develop. Fortunately, this can be broken down into a number of different elements with specific skills which can be worked on.

How you present yourself is a matter of your **non-verbal communication**: the manner in which you communicate using your body in ways that do not involve the words you are speaking. This non-verbal communication can be broken down into a range of specific elements:

- **position**: where you are in the room, and how you position yourself in relation to your audience (which is sometimes also referred to as orientation)

- **gesture**: how you use hand movements to communicate meanings and echo or reinforce the content of the words you are speaking

- **gaze**: where you are looking, and how you use or do not use eye contact to communicate with your audience

KEY TERM

non-verbal communication: communication using the body which does not involve words

position: how a body is positioned in a space, especially in relation to other people

gesture: the use of hand and arm positions and movements to communicate meanings

gaze: the ways in which eye contact is directed towards others in order to communicate

Communication

KEY TERM

paralanguage:
deliberate non-verbal variation of sound from the vocal tract to support and modify verbal communication.

- **paralanguage**: any control you exercise over sound from your vocal tract which does not include words themselves. This may include the volume, pitch and pace (speed) of your voice, and also its intonation. This is the way you might vary volume and pitch to add extra meaning and interest to specific words and phrases.

ACTIVITY 7.06

Over the next week, keep a diary to record ways in which you notice yourself communicating non-verbally. This should not just be academic situations in the classroom, but also how you communicate socially with friends and family and in other everyday transactions, such as going shopping.

Use the headings we have just discussed to make notes, along with a brief note of when the situation took place, what you were doing and who was present:

- position
- gesture
- gaze
- paralanguage

You may want to consider things such as where you placed yourself in the room and in relation to others who were present, hand and arm gestures you used, where and how you directed your gaze, and any noticeable changes in the volume, pace or pitch of your voice at specific moments.

As an additional task, you may decide with another person in your class to make notes on one another's non-verbal communication when you find yourselves in the same location and compare notes on this afterwards.

Reflection: After you have noted these things down, record any ideas you have about why you did this to take account of the situation.

Positioning yourself to give your presentation

Consider how you will position yourself in order to give your presentation. Bear in mind that you will be the only person talking; everyone else in the room is there to listen to you. This means that not only will they need to see your visual aids, but you yourself will need to be

Communication

visible to them, including your gaze and gesture. This will include the person operating the video camera, as the 'camera's eye' represents the position and view of the person who will ultimately be assessing your presentation by watching the video recording.

The following diagram represents one possible version of this arrangement, showing how you might be placed on your own at the front of the room and your audience is grouped at a distance so that all of them, as much as is possible, have an equal view of you and your performance. As part of your planning you may be considering whether to use a lectern, which is a piece of furniture that holds a computer or speaker's notes and you can stand behind to read from. In some circumstances this can be useful, but it could also block your audience's view of your performance and possibly make it more difficult to engage with them.

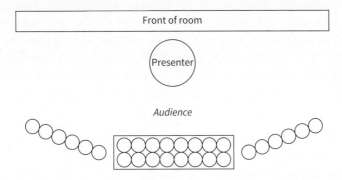

Gestures to support your presentation

It is worth being cautious about planning too many specific hand and arm gestures to support your presentation, as it may make your presentation seem overly elaborate and not effectively add to what you are saying. There are, however, several specific types of gesture which can be helpful when giving a presentation:

- gestures which represent a concrete object to which you are referring (e.g. moving your hands to show its size and shape) or which describe a concept metaphorically (linking specific shapes to individual aspects of the idea, for example)
- gestures which point to a specific part of a slide or other visual aid to indicate that it is being discussed
- rhythmic tapping of a finger, hand or arm to indicate the pace of what you have to say or to highlight key points.

Gaze and giving presentations

Gaze is an important tool for showing your engagement with your audience. Even in conversation with another person, regular (but not continuous) eye contact is crucial in demonstrating that you are paying attention to what they are saying. The same applies to giving a presentation: your audience will not feel you are communicating with them unless you are periodically making eye contact. This is another important reason why you should not read from a pre-prepared script. If you do this then you will not be able to make much, if any, eye contact with your audience.

Discussion point

Can you think of a situation where someone gave you too much or too little eye contact? Think about the effect of this on you, and what they could have done to correct the situation.

Paralanguage and your performance as a presenter

Paralanguage is another aspect of your performance which can be used in specific ways to communicate meanings. There are some more obvious aspects to how paralanguage can help you to present more effectively. For example, you need to speak with sufficient volume for all of your audience to hear you effectively, and you need to maintain a suitable overall pace so that you are not speaking too quickly to be understood, but equally not so slowly that you do not complete your argument in the time that is available. Earlier we gave a general guideline that you could comfortably deliver 110 to 120 words per minute when presenting, but you will need to verify this against what your voice can comfortably deliver and what your audience can absorb.

Beyond this, it is well worth considering and practising your intonation. This is a much more subtle aspect of how you speak, and depends on how the pitch of your voice moves up and down over a phrase, and the way in which that adds emotion and purpose to specific words. It can be very difficult to learn to control, especially if you are a non-native speaker of English. However, there are a number of clear rules you can follow. Falling intonation has a raised pitch at the start of the phrase which lowers towards the end. Rising intonation begins with a lower pitch which rises towards the end.

- Questions which start with *who, what, when, where* or *why* have a falling intonation.
- Questions requiring a yes or no answer have a rising intonation.
- Statements have a falling intonation.
- Lists have a rising intonation for each item except for the final item which has a falling intonation.

Effective and creative performances

Just as the solutions you propose should have an impact on the problem and, if you can, show that you offer a new approach, your presentational methods should also be effective and, ideally, creative. For your visual aids and your personal performance, the test is always that they make a contribution to the argument you are making. This is what makes them effective. **Creativity**, according to the *Cambridge English Dictionary,* is about your ability to produce original and unusual ideas, or to make something new or imaginative. Creativity is always effective because it helps you to make your argument, but beyond this it also looks for new ways of doing so, searching out new approaches to presenting ideas rather than remaining with standard approaches. It is an invitation for you to investigate some of the presentational ideas mentioned in this chapter and use them to forge out in new directions.

> **KEY TERM**
>
> **creativity:** an original, unusual, new or imaginative approach to presenting your arguments

Summary

In this chapter we have:

- looked at what make up the features of an effective presentation
- explored the differences between an effective oral presentation and an essay
- learnt how to prepare effectively for giving presentations
- discussed how to make an effective argument using your oral presentation
- familiarised ourselves with more and less effective ways of using visual aids to support presentations

- outlined how to use gesture, position, gaze and paralanguage to make an engaging and convincing personal performance.

Now that you have completed this chapter, you should be confident about what makes an oral presentation distinctive, and different, from other forms of written communication you have had to undertake for Global Perspectives & Research. In doing so, you should also have been able to link giving a presentation to the core skill of making an argument, and also discovered new and creative ways of producing and supporting your presentation.

Communication

Practising presentations for your team project

This section of the chapter is divided into three: firstly, establishing the effectiveness of your presentation, secondly, developing the effectiveness of your presentation and finally, enhancing the effectiveness of your presentation. Each section is designed to build on the one before. You can either work through each section in turn or choose the section that you feel is at the most appropriate level for you.

You should also see a progression of difficulty through the three levels, but they are also aligned in this chapter to the distinctive skills we have established.

These sections use a variety of topics from the Cambridge International AS & A Level Global Perspectives & Research syllabus.

Establishing effective presentations

Based on what you have read in this chapter, take an inventory of your presentational skills.

- What can you do well already, and what evidence do you have for this from your previous experience with giving presentations?
- What do you still need to work on with your presentational skills and how will you do that?

Developing effective presentations

Plan out the structure of your presentation and make notes on what you will say. Do not try to produce a script, but instead use a mind-map or bullet points to produce a detailed summary which you can then transfer onto cue cards to support your presentation.

Enhancing effective presentations

Choose a type of visual aid or aspect of personal performance from this chapter which you have not tried before. Alternatively, select a method you have used and take advantage of the ideas about where to use it in a new way. How can you develop this to creatively present the explanations and arguments in your presentation?

Chapter 8
Reflection: reflecting on your team project

Learning aims

By the end of this chapter, you should be able to:

- understand the place of reflection in the Global Perspectives & Research course
- describe a range of models of the reflective cycle
- apply the reflective cycle to reflect on your experience of collaboration and what you have learnt in the team project
- evaluate examples of good practice in writing a reflective paper
- produce a reflective paper on your team project experience and on other things you have done.

This chapter will support you with writing reflective papers as part of team projects. Chapters 6, 7 and 8 cover the different aspects of the team project.

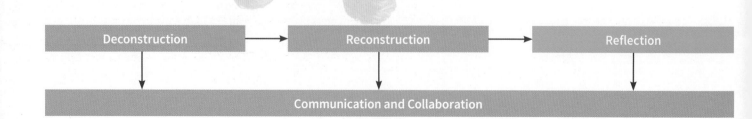

Deconstruction	→	Reconstruction	→	Reflection

Communication and Collaboration

Introduction

We have already encountered reflection in a number of different contexts in this book. **Reflection** (AO2) is one of the three assessment objectives tested by the Global Perspectives & Research course, alongside research, analysis and evaluation (AO1) and communication and collaboration (AO3). There are clear links between the other assessment objectives and the skills you have been developing in the Critical Path. Analysis and evaluation support the process of deconstruction and reconstruction of sources, and in the essay and team project you have been locating those sources yourself by undertaking research. Communication and collaboration have been supporting the path as a whole: communication in the writing of the essay and the delivery of the presentation, and collaboration in your work with your group for the team project and in the other ways you have been working with others to learn things.

Reflection can be seen to lie at the end of the Critical Path in some ways because it is the skill of considering the results of deconstruction and reconstruction so you can make judgements and reach conclusions. However, as the syllabus makes clear, it also has a number of other applications:

KEY TERM

reflection: the evaluation of an action which has already been completed in order to understand it more fully and to undertake it more effectively in the future

- We reflect in order to fully consider and give space to different perspectives, even if they are not our own.
- We reflect so we can consider additional research we could undertake in order to more fully develop our findings (particularly in the essay).
- We reflect in order to consider how our own arguments, judgements and experiences have been changed by engaging with new perspectives.

Reflection, therefore, has a number of important purposes which run through many things we do as part of the Critical Path. It has also occupied a wider role in this book as the reflection points which have frequently followed activities. These have been opportunities to consider what you did or wrote in the activity, to compare this to other possible responses, and to think about how you could have undertaken the activity even more effectively in a different way. This final sense of reflection is also at the heart of the most significant reflective activity you will do as part of Global Perspectives & Research: your reflective paper on the team project. This chapter explores in more precise detail the benefits of this kind of reflection: looking again at what we have already done in order to understand our experiences more fully and do things better in the future. It then looks at some specific methods for reflecting in this way before applying those techniques to the specific subjects for reflection required by the team project's reflective paper and considering some effective examples.

Discussion point

What are the different kinds of reflection, and why are they important?

8.01 The process of reflection

When we reflect in order to look back at what we have done so we can do better in the future, we are setting out to learn from our previous experiences. A number of different writers and thinkers over the years have defined this sort of reflection in slightly different ways:

a 'specialised form of thinking' which moves us from 'routine thinking' to critically considering what we previously took for granted (John Dewey, American philosopher and educational theorist, 1933)

'the process of learning through and from experience' (Linda Finley, Open University, 2008)

Reflection

'the action of turning (back) or fixing the thoughts on some subject; meditation, serious consideration' (*Oxford Shorter English Dictionary*)

Discussion point

Which of the definitions listed above is most useful to you in thinking about reflection, and why?

Reflection involves looking back at something which has already happened:

- It requires us to meditate, or to think carefully and patiently about that completed experience in detail.

- Reflection requires us to consider our experiences critically, questioning what was positive and negative about them.

- When we reflect we should be challenging and questioning what has happened, not merely describing it.

- The purpose of reflection is learning from experience: to be able to do things differently in the future as a response to what has taken place in the past.

Gibbs's reflective cycle

Our discussion of reflection so far shows that it is a series of steps we should undertake after each significant thing we do, and before we do something again. This means that our reflection on past actions makes future actions likely to be more effective, and each time we repeat the process they should get better still. For this reason, people tend to think of reflection as a cycle, where we move from one stage to the next, but the final step then allows us to begin again, even more effectively.

G. Gibbs formalised this in 1988 as a procedure. You can follow it each time you wish to reflect on something that has happened to you, as shown in the diagram below.

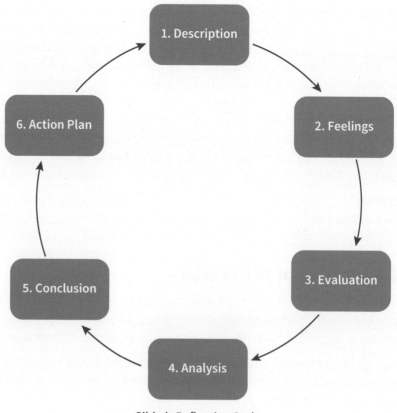

Gibbs's Reflective Cycle

- The first step is to describe as accurately as you can what happened. What did you do? What did other people do? What was said? You need to have an accurate understanding of this in order to apply the remaining stages to the experience.

- Next, consider your feelings about the experience. What did you think about what was being done and said? Here you should describe your emotions, as this is likely to help clarify how you responded to what happened, and the impact of those events on you.

- As is the case at every stage of the Critical Path as a Global Perspectives & Research student, evaluation plays an important role. When you consider what was good or bad about the experience, you are measuring this against the objective you were trying to achieve in the activity. This might be the objective of the group of which you are a member, or of the task you are trying to complete.

- The analysis stage involves making sense of your evaluation by taking a step back and considering the wider context that informs your weighing up of what happened. What additional knowledge or experience do you have which is relevant and can add more information in order to help you in judging the significance of what has occurred? What could you find out?

- With the conclusion stage, you move to decisions on actions. The aim here is to use your reflection so far to identify strengths and weaknesses in your original response. Are there any aspects of what you did that you would repeat? On the other hand, knowing what you do now, what would you not do again?

- The process of reflection should end with a clear action plan. Make a list of steps you will take for the future when you encounter this or similar situations again.

ACTIVITY 8.01

Apply Gibbs's reflective cycle to a situation that has happened to you at school, work or home – but not one of the Global Perspectives & Research tasks. Using the following questions as headings, work your way through each stage of the cycle:

1 What happened?

2 What were you feeling?

3 What was good or bad about the experience?

4 What additional information can you add to make sense of it?

5 What else should you or should you not have done?

6 If the situation happened again, what else would you do?

Writing down your experiences, even if you do so in note form only, is very helpful in clarifying them.

Reflection: The following list contains a possible response to this activity from a student:

1 What happened?

I had to give a presentation in class on a poem we were about to study. I had a lot to say and put it all on the slides I was showing. Although I read from these as quickly as I could, I went over my five minute time allocation and was stopped by my teacher before I had said everything I needed to.

2   What were you feeling?

I felt nervous but excited before starting my presentation. However, as I spoke I felt increasingly anxious about the need to include all of the information I needed and was upset when I suddenly realised I'd run out of time.

3   What was good or bad about the experience?

It was positive that I had managed to gather so much information, and because it was focused on the correct poem it was all relevant. Unfortunately, I had not realised in advance that my presentation was too long and this meant I was not able to deliver all of it to my audience. It was also difficult to remain engaged with them as I was focused on reading the text from my slides.

4   What additional information can you add to make sense of it?

Studies show that the average person can present at between 110 and 120 words per minute. This means I could have delivered a presentation of roughly 600 words within the time I had available. Good practice for giving presentations is to include the presentation content in note form on cue cards or another form of speaker's notes, and to use the slides to enhance this. Again, advice from experienced presenters is that this makes both the presenter and their visual aids more engaging for their audience.

5   What else should you or should you not have done?

I should have planned a presentation within the expected word count for the time I had available. Rehearsing it would have helped me to do that by alerting me to the excessive length. I should have also prepared the content of my presentation using speaker's notes, and saved my slides for high-impact photographs and diagrams.

6   If the situation happened again, what would you do?

My action plan for next time would be to:

- begin by planning my main points, allocating them to each minute of the time I have available

- produce cue cards for each minute of my presentation, with material for up to 120 words of spoken delivery

- produce slides after this to enhance my spoken delivery

- rehearse the presentation several times to ensure it fits within the time allowed

- practise maintaining eye contact with my audience.

Discussion point

Compare your response to the activity with the example given in the reflection point. Consider the extent to which this student's response was reflective, and how it might have helped them to perform more effectively in the future. What are the ways in which following Gibbs's reflective cycle might help you in the same way?

Other models for reflection

It is important to realise that Gibbs's reflective cycle is not the only model for organising reflection. A number of others exist which you may prefer to explore. For example, D.A. Schön (in his 1983 book, *The Reflective Practitioner*) describes reflection as framing our experiences in different ways using the following four-point procedure:

1   Describe the situation.

2   Produce a framework for understanding the situation by making sure you specify where it took place, who was there, and any other factors which may have caused things to happen in the way they did.

3   Shift to a new framework for understanding the situation by bringing in your past knowledge or previous experience that might be relevant.

4   Use the combination of the two frameworks to produce a plan for action to help you deal better with the situation in the future.

In this way, Schön suggests we can reflect effectively by applying new frameworks excessively to the situation. The metaphor here is that by surrounding the situation with new insights and information we can see it in new ways, and recognise aspects of what did or did not work effectively that we may not have seen before.

ACTIVITY 8.02

Review Gibbs's reflective cycle and Schön's model for reflection and answer the following questions:

1   What are the differences and similarities between them?

2   Do you think there are situations where using either one of them might be more or less useful?

Another potential model is offered by N. Hatton and D. Smith in their 1995 article, 'Reflection in Teacher Education'. This contains ideas mainly aimed at teachers who are reflecting on their delivery of learning. However, they can also be applied to anyone who is reflecting on an activity that they have completed. Hatton and Smith say that there are four ways in which it is possible to write about something one has done:

- descriptive writing: a description of the event
- descriptive reflection: an attempt to provide justification for what has been done ('I did this because . . . ')
- dialogic reflection: taking a step back to explore possible alternative courses of action and creating a hypothesis for what might have happened as a result ('Instead of doing this I could have . . . ', 'Taking the alternative course of action may have led to . . . ')
- critical reflection: drawing on wider research and knowledge to explain why things happened in the way they did.

There is no preferred model of reflective theory that it is necessary to learn or use to write your reflective paper. You could choose any of these, or none of them, as long as you use the process of reflection to understand and to evaluate what you have already done in order to act more effectively in the future.

ACTIVITY 8.03

1   Use another of the approaches to reflection to reflect in writing on an experience you have had. It might be the same experience you reflected on using Gibbs's cycle for Activity 8.01 or a different one.

2   Consider the differences and similarities between the approaches to reflection discussed in this section. Do you think any particular one would be more useful for you personally and why?

Reflecting on the team project

This requires you to apply the skills of reflection to your experience of the team project. When you do this, you will be reflecting on two particular aspects:

- your collaboration with the other members of your team
- your learning from the team project.

You should include a summary of your team's overall, agreed solution that you discussed at the end of the process, but the focus for your reflection should be the process of team work and your own learning. It is this which will enable you to evaluate and make judgements, and your work on this will be assessed.

8.02 Reflecting on collaboration

The first area on which you should reflect is your experience of working in your team when working on the team project. Chapter 6 discusses a number of aspects of this collaborative process and shows that the most important aspect of any group is its intended outcome. When we assess whether a group has succeeded or failed, we are looking at whether or not it has achieved its intended outcome. This will be your judgement on your group's collaboration. As a task-focused group, it is very important to have your group's task at the front of your mind when performing this judgement.

In the team project, this is what your group must do:

1   Identify a suitable local problem which also has global significance which the whole group can investigate.

2   Research the problem to gather a sufficient amount of evidence about it.

3   Allocate each member of the group a complementary perspective on the problem, so that they can go on to conduct their own research and develop their own solutions for their individual presentation.

4   Come together at the end to agree a group solution.

Each aspect of the group's collaboration which you evaluate must be judged against these objectives. This means you will be first making a judgement about whether each of the objectives was finally achieved. Then you will be identifying the causes for that success or failure. Some of these causes, as we saw in Chapter 6, will be related to the processes by which the group operated. Others will be due to the actions of members of the group. Here are some of the possible factors you will have to consider:

Issues related to group processes

- how the group was created
- how the group was led
- the size of the group
- who was allocated a role within the group
- what activities individual members, and the group as a whole, undertook.

Issues related to group members

- who generated ideas, and who listened to those ideas
- who ensured the actions which were agreed were implemented
- who created systems for ensuring everyone worked together efficiently and how
- who motivated the group and who decreased motivation
- who made a contribution and who did not.

ACTIVITY 8.04

Use the issues listed above to make your own list of what you think were the key issues for your group in undertaking the team project.

In order to carry out this task, you may find it helpful to re-read Chapter 6, which discusses issues affecting collaboration in much more detail. It is important to remember, however, that this chapter was written to prepare you for the group task, whereas now you are reviewing it once it has been completed.

When you have made your own list you may find it useful to discuss it with another member of your team. How does theirs compare? If they have come up with a different list of issues, then talk about what the group's objectives were and see if you agree.

Using the reflective cycle to reflect on collaboration

It is possible to think critically in a general way about the issues which are relevant to your team's work as a group, and use the results of this to write that part of your reflective paper. However, your results are likely to be much more effective if you use one of the approaches to reflection outlined in Section 8.01. For example, this is one student's reflection on their collaborative experience using Gibbs's reflective cycle:

1   **What happened?**

I was allocated into a team with two other students. We met as a group to decide on the problem we'd focus on, discussing what was affecting our local area. I mainly discussed this with Jill because Joe and Pete did not make many contributions. We decided to focus on access to healthcare as our families had both experienced issues with this. We allocated everyone an approach to this topic, including Joe and Pete. After this we did not meet as a group again, apart from at the very end. When we did, we found out that Joe and Pete had swapped economic and technological solutions between them, and Jill had decided to compare political solutions to accessing healthcare in a different part of the world.

2   **What were you feeling?**

I felt disappointed and a little angry with Joe and Pete for not taking an active role in our group, or coming up with any ideas of their own. It was also surprising that the other members of my group had changed their approaches, which I only found out after their presentations. Feeling that we were not quite in control of our project as a group caused some anxiety in me.

3   **What was good or bad about the experience?**

I was pleased that we did identify a common topic and developed contrasting perspectives which were presented. However, it was not so good that not all group members participated in the process of selecting a topic or approach, and our failure to meet was also a problem. This meant that most group members ended up changing approaches and solutions without any reference to each other.

4   **What additional information can you add to make sense of it?**

Where we succeeded and failed, it was because of the roles taken by different members of the group. Jill and I took on Albrecht's role of ideas person, as we worked to generate ideas for the rest of the group. However, no one ensured this was done (Albrecht's action role), and positive group roles were distinctly lacking. In Albrecht's terms, Joe and Pete were uncommitted to the group.

5   **What should you or should you not have done?**

To summarise:

- We should have come up with a schedule for meeting regularly.
- We should have minuted agreed actions.
- Someone should have monitored to see what was completed.
- Jill and I should not have imposed a problem and approaches on others.

6   **If the situation happened again, what would you do?**

If doing this again, I would try to put together a group sharing a common interest and we would spend longer discussing possible approaches and deciding on the roles and procedures we were going to adopt as a group before getting on with our own research. We would also extend the group activity over a longer timescale to allow for discussion and negotiation of our approaches.

As can be seen from this example, effective reflection does not depend on the group activity being completely, or even partially, successful in achieving its objectives. What matters is your ability to identify the detail of what has happened, evaluate strengths and weaknesses, and use a wider context of knowledge to plan more effective action for the future.

ACTIVITY 8.05

Use Gibbs's headings to reflect on your own team-project group experience and make notes. These should be detailed, with specific examples from what you and other group members did.

Writing up your reflection on collaboration

Once you have used a reflective framework to record notes on your team's collaborative performance, you will use that as material for your reflective paper. A reflective paper is an argument giving evidence for your conclusions about your group's performance, although it

Reflection

is still very much focused on your personal experience and response to the situation. This can be seen in this extract from a reflective paper which discusses the collaborative experience:

> I found it enjoyable to have only one other group member, as it made the presentation process much more simplified in how we were able to communicate and the amount of work we had. Peter and I decided on our problem statement by consensus and our solutions developed from this. Having a friendship which preceded our task-focused group meant we did not have to worry about the odd honeymoon period that every group experiences as they get to know each other before beginning to work.

> A clear limitation of having minimal group members, however, is the narrowed perspective which this gave us on our work. While we believe that our solution is the best solution that could possibly be formulated in the time available, it is necessarily a selection from the narrow set of perspectives we had. This issue could be remedied with the addition of more group members, with each individual being able to contribute to a larger discussion.

This analysis contains the following elements from Gibbs's reflective cycle:

- what happened ('only one other group member', 'decided on our problem statement by consensus')
- feelings ('I found it enjoyable')
- what was good or bad about the group work ('a clear limitation . . . ')
- additional information (the reference to the problems which typically accompany group formation)
- what should have been done and future plans ('This issue could be remedied with the addition of more group members').

The material for reflection has been taken from a set of structured notes and reorganised into an argument about the strengths and weaknesses of the group activity which is focused, precise and evidenced.

Discussion point
How would you turn the notes you made from Activity 8.05 into a formal argument of your own? What would stay the same and what would be different?

8.03 Reflecting on learning

Collaboration is not the only focus for a reflective paper. You are also asked to reflect on what you have learnt from participating in the team project. If we think about learning here, we might consider it as a three-stage process:

- Stage 1: the knowledge, ideas and feelings about the issue, problem and possible solutions before starting on the group work and discussion
- Stage 2: the knowledge, ideas and feelings about the issue, problem and possible solutions after completing the team project, having undertaken all the research and work in groups, and having seen the presentations of other group members
- Between stages 1 and 2: the experiences of change, and new information and insights gained from research done and other group members in order to get from stage 1 to stage 2.

Because you are reflecting on this, it is not sufficient simply to have learnt something. You need to be able to identify exactly what you have learnt, where the learning has come from and what the significance of that learning was.

ACTIVITY 8.06

Consider another subject you are learning. This might be another International A Level or something you are learning for a hobby or other leisure activity. Make a list of examples of things you learn, where that learning comes from and why it is significant.

Reflection: Learning might come from a variety of sources:

- books, newspapers and magazines, other websites
- questions and surveys with groups of people
- individual conversations with others
- watching someone explain an idea or argument.

When you think about the significance of what you have learnt, you might want to consider:

- whether you have done something differently as a result of the learning, or might do so in the future
- whether what you have learnt changes the whole way you see what you are doing, or only a part of it.

It would also be good to consider your new learning as another perspective, using the Critical Path. This means you could make notes on what you have learnt under these headings:

- What does the new learning lead you to conclude, and how is that different from what you might have concluded before?
- What are the reasons used to support that conclusion – is there anything striking or different about these?
- Does the new learning use new or different evidence, especially types of evidence you are not used to?
- Where does the new learning come from – is it a context with which you had not previously engaged?
- What does the new learning seem to assume? Remember that assumptions are unstated reasons which are needed to support the conclusions reached. Have you needed to change your own assumptions as a result?

Using models of reflection to reflect on your learning

Just as with reflection on collaboration, it is important to use a systematic approach to organise your ideas about what you have learnt as you reflect on your learning. You will need to consider which model, approach or set of headings you are most comfortable with. The approach you used when reflecting on your work in a group may not be the most appropriate one to take for reflection on your learning.

At this point, it is useful to remind ourselves of Schön's model for reflection, which was introduced in Section 8.01:

1 Describe the situation.

2 Produce a framework for understanding the situation by making sure you specify where it took place, who was there, and any other factors which may have caused things to happen in the way they did.

Reflection

3 Shift to a new framework for understanding the situation by bringing in your past knowledge or previous experience that might be relevant.

4 Use the combination of the two frameworks to produce a plan for action to help you deal better with the situation in the future.

In some ways, this is a more challenging approach to apply than that of Gibbs, as it does not specify what the 'framework' might be in steps 3 and 4. However, this also means it is more flexible, and allows you to specify what is most appropriate for the learning experience you have had.

Here is how we might apply Schön's model to learning gained as part of the team project:

1 Describe the situation.

In our project we decided to focus on the income gap between the rich and poor in our local area, in other parts of the United States and in other areas of the world. Within our group we investigated a number of contrasting approaches to closing this gap which had very different assumptions behind them.

2 Provide an initial framework for understanding the situation.

When starting on this project, I assumed that economic gaps within society were a political problem, and that it was the responsibility of the government to take action to close them. This meant I focused on evidence from the context of economists who saw changing the supply of income as being the solution. This meant that I argued for raising the minimum wage and increasing income tax on the wealthy in my presentation. The second part of my solution involves taking direct action to redistribute wealth from the richer members of society to poorer ones.

3 Shift to a new framework.

Although I assumed that direct, government-led redistributive action was the only solution to inequality, I was surprised when Ellen, the other member of my team, argued for a free trade solution. This involved an opposite approach to mine: reducing taxes on businesses to give them incentives to raise wages for their workers. I was especially struck by her argument for this in her presentation, as she showed that it would require minimal changes to the current regulatory framework without the risks associated with significantly higher taxes. I was also surprised by the evidence which emerged from the research we did as a group: tax cuts in the US undertaken by the Reagan administration were successful in increasing Gross Domestic Product, and free trade has also been shown to have increased the quality and range of goods in India and Japan.

4 Use the combination of frameworks to suggest a better way forward.

I still believe both approaches have their merits: tax breaks and trade liberalisation have been shown to be more efficient solutions with a lower cost. However, their use assumes that companies will respond by redirecting income to increasing people's wages, and this may not always be the case. However, as a result of what I have learnt from my team project, I would be prepared to take this approach as an initial solution to the problem before changing government policy.

As with your reflection on collaboration, you would then write up these notes as an argument for the strengths and weaknesses of your knowledge and assumptions at the start of your process and the new learning you encountered. As this example shows, that learning can come from what you hear from other group members, what you learn from the research you undertake, or a combination of both. It is also equally possible to come to different conclusions about the value of that learning:

- You may feel that the new learning you have encountered shows that your previous way of thinking should be abandoned.
- You may find that having learnt about alternative approaches, your initial solution is still the most effective one.
- Your final position may combine elements of your existing thinking with new learning.

Any of these three positions is equally justifiable. The point is that you reflect on which one you wish to adopt, use a systematic framework for doing so and justify your final position with reasons and evidence.

Discussion Point

What do you feel you have learnt from doing the team project? Has using a model of reflection helped you to get a clearer view of this?

Summary

In this chapter we have:

- described the place of reflection in the Global Perspectives & Research course and the Critical Path as a whole, and explained how it can be applied specifically as part of the team project
- explained a range of models of reflection, starting with Gibbs's reflective cycle
- applied the reflective cycle and other models of reflection so you have been able to reflect on your experience of collaboration and what you have learnt in the team project
- evaluated examples of good practice in writing a reflective paper
- produced a reflective paper on your team project experience and on other things you have done.

The ability to reflect is a crucial skill. It helps us to make sense of experiences we have had, and use that to change and improve our behaviour in the future. Models of reflection give us structured ways to do this, which we can test out. By the end of this chapter you should be able to undertake the written reflection that is required in response to your team project experience. However, in reflecting on lessons which would make you a better collaborator and learner, you also have the ability to apply reflection to improve your performance in other areas of your life and learning. This will include the research you do for your research report (dealt with in the final chapter) as well as the studies and other activities you undertake in the future.

Reflection

Practising reflection for the team project

This section of the chapter is divided into three: firstly, establishing reflection, secondly, developing reflection and finally, enhancing reflection. Each section is designed to build on the one before. You can either work through each section in turn or choose the section that you feel is at the most appropriate level for you.

You should also see a progression of difficulty through the three levels, but they are also aligned in this chapter to the distinctive skills we have established.

Establishing reflection

You may not have previously considered that reflection is something that is useful or necessary in your everyday experiences. Before thinking about specific topics you are looking at for your team project or elsewhere in your learning at school, try taking time to reflect on things that happen to you during the day. Use this simple three-point plan to take notes at the end of the day:

1 What did I do today?
2 What could I have done differently?
3 What would the result of this have been, and what should I do differently tomorrow?

After you have done this for a week, read back through your entries. How has your behaviour changed and do you think reflection might be a useful thing for you to do in the future?

Developing reflection

Journalling is another common reflective practice. Try writing a journal for a period of one or two weeks. You can do this in a notebook or on a computer document. At the end of each day, use Gibbs, Schön or another specific framework for reflection to choose a critical incident from the day and reflect on it. See how this develops your effectiveness in reflecting.

Enhancing reflection

You are now ready to undertake each of the stages and produce your reflective paper. Make sure you begin by taking notes using a combination of reflective approaches (one for collaboration and another perhaps for learning) and also state your group solution. Use your notes to write up an argument for the effectiveness of your group work and the significance of your learning.

Chapter 9
The research report

```
Deconstruction  →  Reconstruction  →  Reflection
         ↓               ↓                ↓
                   Communication
```

Introduction

The research report is the final and largest piece of work you will produce for Global Perspectives & Research. It is required if you wish to complete the full A Level and makes up half of the marks, as much as the written paper, essay and team project combined. Because of this, however, it also builds on what you have done in those first three components, bringing together all of the skills and experiences you have had. We can see it as the destination located at the end of the Critical Path, but also as the combination of all the stages along that road. You will need to have fully developed your ability to deconstruct, reconstruct and reflect, bringing them together in your extended written communication in your final report. Your collaborative skills are not assessed directly but will also come in useful, as you work with your teacher as research mentor, meeting them regularly throughout the course and having a formal interview with them at the end.

In this chapter, we will first outline exactly what the research report requires, and how it is assessed. Following that, you will have the opportunity to reflect on the skills you have been developing while working towards the written paper, essay and team project. This is important, as all of these skills will be central to your work on the report. You will then learn how and why you should maintain a research log, and what kind of issues you need to consider depending on whether you have chosen a research topic in the arts, sciences or social sciences. After that we will examine, with examples of effective work, how to write the report, and how to apply your knowledge of citation and reference to this piece of work. Finally, we will turn to your life after and outside of Global Perspectives & Research: how the report is a bridge to your other A Levels, and to what you will do after your A Levels, especially your studies at university.

9.01 What is the research report?

The research report is a piece of written work which is the fourth component of your A Level in Global Perspectives & Research. The marks you will receive from it will make up 50% of your final qualification and it is also a required element for the A Level if you will be working towards that, rather than just the AS. Because of this, it is a substantial as well as exciting piece of work.

The skills needed for the report

The report has a number of similarities with the work you have already produced, or may currently be producing, for Global Perspectives & Research:

- It uses the skills of the Critical Path.
- It is a written argument in the form of an essay.
- That argument must be supported by evidence.
- You will be using sources and recording them in a bibliography.
- You will be developing your own question and answering it.
- The question must be organised as a debate which involves identifying and evaluating more than one perspective.
- It must also allow you to reach a final judgement in response to the question.
- You will be doing research and finding your own sources.
- Your work will also include a written reflection evaluating your progress, and there is also an oral component.

However, it also has a number of differences. Some of these are new things you will need to be able to do, and others develop and extend skills you have already:

- For the report, you will be writing a maximum of 5,000 words.
- Your question can be based on any academic topic of your choice.
- That question will need to be supported by a formal proposal which must be approved before you proceed with researching and writing your report.
- Your teacher will support you with developing your research and writing skills, and in the writing of your question, as well as questioning you about your progress. However, you will be expected to work much more independently than you did for the other parts of the course.
- You will need to reflect on your work in a much more detailed way than you did for your reflective paper on your team project by using a research log. You will not give a presentation but will need to give an oral explanation of the work you have done at the end of the process in a spoken interview with your teacher.

ACTIVITY 9.01

Before starting on your work for the report, it is good idea to assess how you have already developed the skills and attitudes you will need from other parts of the course and elsewhere.

Make a copy of the table below and complete it by filling in evidence of where you think you have already done each of the skills and attitudes listed. Where you think you have managed it consistently, write C. If you think you have been able to do it partially (but still need some development) then write P. For those skills and attitudes which you do not think you have acquired at all yet, write X.

Progress assessment	
Skill or attitude	**How have you managed it?**
Researching sources	
Evaluating sources and evidence	
Evaluating arguments	
Writing a question which focuses on a debate	
Identifying contrasting perspectives	
Citing and referencing sources	
Writing arguments in essays	
Working independently	
Reflecting on what you have done	

Producing targets

Now you have assessed your starting points, you will be in a position to create some targets for yourself so you can produce the strongest possible report. These should be **SMART** targets. These are:

- **Specific**: You should describe one particular thing you want to do.
- **Measurable**: You need to be able to say how you will check you have done it.

- **Achievable**: You will need to be able to achieve it given the resources and capabilities you have (or could develop).
- **Relevant**: It needs to be relevant to what you will need to do in order to successfully produce your report.
- **Time-based**: It needs to be something you can do in a specific period of time, and one which matches up with your deadlines for producing the report.

Reflection: Think about opportunities you will have for practising, improving and checking these skills, either in work you are doing for other parts of the Global Perspectives & Research courses, other subjects you are studying or your work for the report itself.

How the report is assessed

The assessment and marking criteria for the report are listed in the Cambridge International AS & A Level Global Perspectives & Research syllabus. Unlike the first three components, the report will be marked by your teacher using these criteria and standards set out in the syllabus to ensure that your work is marked to the same standard as that submitted by students at other schools. A sample of work from your school will be checked to ensure that this is the case. It is also useful for you as a student to consider how your work will be assessed, as these criteria describe the skills you will be working on developing.

Research

You will need to:

- develop a suitable research question
- manage your research appropriately with a plan
- record what you do using your research log.

Analysis and evaluation

You will need to:

- select relevant sources
- extract concepts, arguments and evidence from them which are convincing and relevant to your argument
- identify, break down and evaluate a range of relevant perspectives on each side of your debate
- evaluate the methods you use to research your chosen subject area
- evaluate and bring together arguments, evidence and perspectives in order to reach your own supported conclusions.

Reflection

You will need to:

- reflect on the nature of your research, including the limitations of what you could have achieved using the time, methods and sources available
- reflect on how your own views and knowledge have changed and developed as you have done your research and written the report.

Deconstruction

Reconstruction

Reflection

Communication

Communication

You will need to:

- use appropriate language and terminology accurately in your report
- structure your report effectively
- use a method of citing and referencing your sources accurately and effectively
- communicate orally with your teacher at the end of the process in a clear way to explain the research you have done.

We will refer back to these skills, explaining them further, in the rest of this chapter.

9.02 Choosing and developing your topic

One of the distinctive features of the report is that you can choose any academic topic you like. Unlike with the written paper, you will not have questions set for you, but nor will you have to choose from issues relevant to the syllabus topics, as you did for the essay and team project. Instead, the subject of your report should focus on the skills which you have built up by following the Global Perspectives & Research course. This means that:

- it should allow you to focus on a debate between perspectives
- you should have to research evidence and arguments from a range of sources
- your report should ask and answer a question
- it should be based on something **academic**, not personal interests or hobbies.

KEY TERM

academic: related to something studied at school or college, or related to studying and thinking, not practical activity or personal interests

---

ACTIVITY 9.02

Starting points for a project like the report are often the most difficult things to think about. One strategy is to consider an item which interests you. This might be:

- an article you have read from a newspaper, magazine or academic journal
- another textbook or perhaps novel you have looked at which interests you
- a documentary video, television news report, picture or musical recording
- a sample of material, such as a rock, soil, chemical or other material, natural or artificially made.

The advantage of doing this is that it allows you to select it as the first possible source on which you are working as part of the work for your report. To help you select a possible item, make notes on the following:

- an explanation of what the item is and why it interests you
- questions you might want to ask about it, or questions you think it might help to answer
- any other items you might read or collect to go with it, especially if it might help you to set up a dialogue or debate between them.

Once you have done this, you might want to show your item to your class or another group of students and talk through what you have written on it in your notes. Anything other people then ask you about your item might help you to clarify your ideas.

Discussion point

If you are having trouble choosing something for your report, then you could carry out a short assessment of your interests to go along with the skills assessment you did for Activity 9.01. This would involve answering these questions:

- What is my favourite A Level or other school subject?
- What was the most interesting piece of academic work I have completed in the last three months?
- What am I considering studying at university, or what area of work would I like to go into for a career?

By doing this, you may be able to identify a broad area of interest which will motivate you to carry out the research for your report. Motivation is very important here, as you will need to keep going for some time on your own in order to successfully complete the report.

Focusing on a suitable debate

As well as a suitable interest and item, or other source, you will also need to find a debate. There needs to be more than one possible approach, answer or interpretation from which you can then develop different perspectives. This might be the case in a number of ways:

- If you have chosen a novel, there may be a number of different readings of its main theme, characterisation, or use of language which produce contrasting conclusions.
- A historical event, or document, might have a number of different interpretations based on historians' reading of the evidence.
- There might be contrasting models being used to explain a natural phenomenon, such as the expansion of the Universe or the movement of fluids, each of which has strengths and weaknesses.
- There may be contrasting approaches to the treatment of a mental health condition, such as depression, some involving medication but others relying on talking-based approaches like psychoanalysis or counselling.

Projects in science or mathematics, in particular, which would require you to measure or map out the evidence for something to explain what is going on would be less suitable. It is important that you are able to investigate contrasting arguments and link them to different perspectives. As in the other parts of the Global Perspectives & Research course, you are still looking for differences in:

- where the sources are from (their context)
- arguments
- evidence
- assumptions.

If you are interested in a particular subject area, then it is a good idea to talk to a teacher of that subject, or other students studying it, to explore what the debates might be, and the different assumptions they have, or arguments they make.

Reflection:
Consider the other subjects you are doing. Which topics or areas from each of them would meet the criteria for the report, and which would not?

From discovery to first proposal

Once you have identified an item as your first source, and had the opportunity to discuss its possibilities with other people, including the different debates around it, the next step is to formalise these ideas using a structure which will ensure you are producing work which is appropriate for the purpose of the report and the skills it tests.

KEY TERM

research proposal:
a short written summary of the intended content of your research report, with the areas your research will cover

You can do this by creating a **research proposal**, which is a written summary of what you think your report might do under some suitable headings. To do this you will need to do some more reading and thinking to find additional resources, testing out and developing the ideas you had from your first item and the feedback you received on it.

Your proposal will start with a question. This does not have to be very precise or well-developed at this stage, but it should be the same type of question as you produced for the essay: an *interrogative*, which requests an answer and suggests there could be alternatives, rather than an *imperative*, which is an instruction (to find something in a source, as you might do in the written paper), or a *declarative*, a statement of a problem, like the one you addressed in the team project. Like your work for the essay, it should also clearly focus on a debate and lead to an answer where you can make a judgement.

ACTIVITY 9.03

It is now time for you to put down your first developed ideas for your report in writing. This will include a question and some details to explain and justify it. Try doing this using these headings:

- My question
- Why it is an important question to answer
- How I would answer this question now
- Any other possible answers to the question
- Sources I can use which I have found so far

Reflection: By using these headings, you can test out whether your first idea for a report fulfils the requirements of the report by having a question, being a question that is worth your researching and answering, has at least one possible answer, and some alternative answers, so there is a debate, and is based on evidence from sources.

Set out below is one student's effort at filling in the headings to show what might be possible:

My question: Is globalisation economically good for developed countries?

Why it is an important question to answer

This subject is discussed a lot at the moment as an issue in economics, so I know it is possible to have a good debate about it. I think that with all of this there may be some complex arguments for me to explore. As a student studying both geography and economics, this also seems to combine them in some really interesting ways. I've already found out that similar questions have been discussed in well-known books by famous authors, so reading these will be really interesting and allow me to develop my research further.

How I would answer this question now

At the moment, it seems really obvious to me that globalisation is really good for developed countries. I think it might also help countries that are developing at the moment, as it will give them the opportunity to become wealthier through global trade. Globalisation means that we have more access to goods, information and services, and this is bound to make us better off.

Any other possible answers to the question

There might be some downsides. I have read some economists argue that as countries like China become wealthier through global trade, this might threaten the economies of established Western countries like the US and UK.

Sources I can use which I have found so far

Thomas Friedman, The Lexus and the Olive Tree *(2012)*

Peter Dicken, Global Shift *7th ed. (2014)*

Jim O'Neill, 'Globalisation has made the world a better place', The Guardian *18 January 2017, https://www.theguardian.com/business/2017/jan/18/globalisation-world-trade-asia-global-poverty*

Creatively developing your proposal

Once you have a first draft of your proposal, it is really important to continue to develop it – to get feedback from your teacher and other students, and also look for different ways in which you can add to and improve it. One way in which you can do this is to present your proposal as a poster for your teacher and other students. In Section 7.05, posters were discussed as a possible visual aid for supporting your individual presentation as part of the team project. You can now draw on those skills to present your ideas and arguments for your report. An effective poster allows you to:

- visually organise the required elements of your report
- share your findings directly with others
- explore, experiment with and develop your ideas.

ACTIVITY 9.04

Using the project proposal you have already set out in Activity 9.03, use the opportunity of creating a poster to develop it further. In order to do this you will have to be critical about your question in particular: is it really an interrogative? Does it focus on a debate? Are there key concepts which I can use my question to highlight? Can I reflect further on the importance and motivation of the issue I have selected? Have I located further, even more relevant sources?

Once you have done this, produce a poster using the guidelines in Section 7.05. It should include:

- your question
- clarification of your key terms
- a summary of the debate
- reflection on why it motivates you
- details of the sources you plan to use.

You will find it very useful to re-read Sections 4.03 and 4.04 at this point, as they focus on writing questions and clarifying terms. The guidance given there on framing appropriate questions, and the techniques for reducing ambiguity and vagueness in your question's terms, still applies here.

Research Report Proposal Poster

The Debate

- Some people think that greater freedom of information, liberalised finance and other measures lead to further development and advancements into new markets for the MEDCs.

- Alternatively, others believe that because globalisation results in the growth of new superpowers like China and India, this could cause the economic dominance of such 'Western' countries as the UK and USA to be compromised.

- This is a good debate because economists and other specialists have a range of different views, showing the varied possibilities of this question.

Key Terms

- **globalisation:** 'a situation in which available goods and services, or social and cultural influences, gradually become similar in all parts of the world' and 'the increase of trade around the world' (Cambridge Dictionary, online)

- **economically efficient (Pareto efficiency):** a situation where 'there is no other allocation in which some other individual is better off and no individual is worse off' (University of Toronto)

- **developed country:** 'A country that allows all its citizens to enjoy a free and healthy life in a safe environment' (Kofi Annan, Former UN General Secretary)

Is globalisation economically efficient for developed countries?

Sources

There is a wide range of sources on the topic of globalisation: it is a popular topic. Here are my starting points:

- Thomas Friedman, The Lexus and the Olive Tree (2012) Peter Dicken, Global Shift 7th ed. (2014)
- Jim O'Neil, 'Globalisation has made the world a better place', The Guardian, 18 January 2017, https://www.theguardian.com/business/2017/jan/18/globalisation-world-trade-asia-global-poverty

Furthermore, many books and journals have been based on the topic of globalisation by some of the most reputable authors, These give detailed expressions about globalisation and the author's opinion on it.

Motivation

This topic combines my two main areas of interest – human geography and economics. Globalisation is a central concern in both of these subject areas, and after studying a range of arguments around this I would like to explore it more closely. The concept of globalisation interests me, and I would very much like to answer the central area for enquiry when I read about this – is it a good thing for developed countries?

Formally submitting the Outline Proposal Form

Once you have fully developed your proposal using your initial headings and then a poster, it will be time to formally submit this for consideration by using the Outline Proposal Form (OPF). This is a required step, so you must do it. However, it is still very much part of a process of dialogue which has involved your teacher and fellow students, and will continue after you have received this feedback.

What the OPF does require you to do is to express your proposal in a formal, discursive manner. This means that you are making an argument, in full sentences and paragraphs, that your research proposal meets the requirements of the report. This means that you will need to show that your question is focused on a debate which you can explore and answer in the 5,000 words you have available and that there are sources you can find and evaluate in detail.

Discussion point

When you get feedback, consider it carefully and discuss it with your teacher, thinking about what actions you should take as a result. This is an important part of the research process.

9.03 The research process and log

From your first thoughts about your report you will have had to embark on a process of research: finding sources and making biased decisions on what you have found. Those decisions will have helped you decide which sources to look at next, and also shaped the way in which you have defined and expressed the question you are researching, and what this focuses on.

Everything you have written down and presented about your research so far will have helped with this: from your thoughts about the first item or source you found, to the initial headings of your first research proposal, to the poster you presented and the Outline Proposal Form. Doing this was really important because it allowed you to record and reflect on what you had done, in order to decide what you need to do next.

The research log provides an opportunity for you to continue to do this throughout the process of producing your report. On the one hand, it will allow you to demonstrate that you are able to reflect, both here and in your report itself, on the scale of your research and on what you have been learning from doing it, much as you did on your learning from the team project in the reflective paper. On the other hand, however, it will be a tool which is useful in supporting your research itself, as you will use it to record each of the sources you have found and where they will fit into your thinking, as well as the decisions which have sharpened and focused your question and argument. Together with the notes you make on individual sources, and the planning of its structure, this will help you to successfully write your report.

What is in your research log?

The research log does not have a fixed, required format. Instead it is an opportunity for you to record details of what you are researching as your project develops. Like a diary, it should record developments over time, so every time you write in it you should record the date. This will help you to see how your thinking has developed and also distinguish things you have found at an early stage of your research from your thinking later on as you come to write the report. One other constraint is that it needs to be electronically submitted as an appendix to your report, so you will need to type it on a computer rather than producing it by hand.

Your research log might include:

- reflections on significant decisions you make about the scope, focus and direction of your report, or things you have found out. (When you write these up you may wish to use one of the standard models for reflection, such as Gibbs's reflective cycle, described in Chapter 8.)
- new versions of your research question, or other ideas supporting each of your developed research proposals, and notes on why they have changed
- lists of things to do or to check
- references for sources you have found, and brief notes on why they are useful (although you will still need to produce detailed notes on the sources you think you may wish to use directly in your report).

Extract from an example reflective log

Date: 23 January 2017 — date

Came across idea of neuroplasticity in my biology lesson – idea that mental capacity can be increased through training the brain.

Searched for this using Google and found:

Norman Doidge: the man teaching us to change our minds, *The Observer*, 8 February 2015 (https://www.theguardian.com/science/2015/feb/08/norman-doidge-brain-healing-neuroplasticity-interview) - argues that mental training programmes can change structure of the brain. See separate notes

References two books I can also read:

Norman Doidge, *The Brain that Changes Itself* (2008)

Norman Doidge, *The Brain's Way of Healing* (2016)

details of sources found and comment on them

Date: 24 January 2017

Spoke to teacher. Explained what I had found out about neuroplasticity. Was asked if this was a debate and remembered from biology lesson that opposing explanation is that intelligence is genetically determined. Need to remember to look for sources to support counter-arguments too. — reflective comment

Found this:

Alison Motluk, IQ is inherited, suggests twin study, *New Scientist*, 5 November 2001 (https://www.newscientist.com/article/dn1520-iq-is-inherited-suggests-twin-study/)

Studies of identical twins seem to show high degree of heritability of brain structures and IQ. See separate notes.

ACTIVITY 9.05

Write a log for a day at school, recording what happens in your lessons, other work you complete and learning decisions you make in the same format as the example given in this section.

9.04 The research process and research methodologies

As we have already seen, your report is not limited to one of the topics from the Cambridge International AS & A Level Global Perspectives & Research syllabus. You are invited instead to research debates from any academic area you choose, drawing together interests you have from other subjects you are studying, and your plans for university. This diversity means you do not just have to consider contrasting perspectives within the issue you have selected, where each side may differ in their arguments, evidence, assumptions and context. You also have to consider what is distinctive about the subject area from which it comes, and the implications of this for how you conduct your research and write your project.

From themes to subject domains: developing the idea of a perspective

When you were developing questions and organising sources for your essay and team project, you used the themes listed in the Cambridge International AS & A Level Global Perspectives & Research syllabus to help you to work out contrasting perspectives on your issue. These seven themes were as follows:

- culture
- economics
- environment
- ethics
- politics
- science
- technology.

Each theme involved a focus on a distinctive type of evidence, usually involved arguments which contrasted with the other themes, relied on sources from a similar context and made assumptions which differed from every other theme. Because of this, themes were good starting points for defining alternative perspectives, and identifying more than one thematic approach to the same issue was a useful starting point for defining alternative perspectives, either to be explored in the essay or adopted in the team project and contrasted with the perspectives taken up by other team members or found in your research.

The nature of the issue you are likely to have chosen for the report is somewhat different. It represents a good opportunity not to be constrained by the list of Global Perspectives & Research topics as well as the seven themes. Instead you are invited to explore an academic issue from any subject you are studying at school, or a combination of more than one subject, or perhaps an aspect of a subject you would like to study at university. Surprisingly, this openness and flexibility of choice mean that the report question you focus on in the end is likely to be much more thematically narrow. This can be seen if we organise the following list of student report questions using some of the existing Global Perspectives & Research themes:

Culture
- Is the term 'God' enough to prove God's existence?
- What was the key factor behind Constantine's decision to convert to Christianity?
- Is the framework of war poetry the best way to characterise the work of Wilfred Owen?

Economics
- Is globalisation economically efficient for developed countries?

Deconstruction
Reconstruction
Reflection
Communication

Environment

- Are international carbon reduction agreements the best solution to climate change?

Science

- Is taking an animal out of its natural habitat the most effective method of conservation?
- Does dark matter exist?
- Is there any place for valence bond theory in modern organic chemistry?

Each of these questions has clear alternative perspectives but is clearly located in a single thematic area. For example, those arguing for or against the existence of dark matter, or the use of valence bond theory to explain atomic bonding, would all be operating within a scientific perspective. The opposing arguments about the economic efficiency of globalisation would all be economic.

KEY TERM

methodology: the study of the most appropriate methods to use to research and develop knowledge in a specific subject area

What is required is a different way of organising the contrasting arguments, evidence, assumptions and contexts you will find in the various perspectives present in your chosen debate. This is done by organising your perspectives using a specific **methodology**.

This methodology is different to the methods you are using to undertake research. These were discussed in Chapter 3 and include using key terms to locate sources using library catalogues and search engines, making lists of sources and selecting ones to read from these, as well as using reading techniques for extracting relevant parts of each text and guidance on note-taking to record arguments, evidence and other material about each source. As you work on your report, you will be using and developing exactly the same skills in order to do your research, and recording this in your research log. The only difference is that for your report you will be spending longer doing the research (months rather than weeks), there will be more sources to find and organise, and you will have to manage this process much more for yourself, with less frequent support and checking from your teacher.

Methodology, on the other hand, is the study or understanding of methods. It is what comes from a consideration of why a specific set of methods is appropriate for an academic subject or area of study. Methodology considers some of the following questions:

- Why do I select some kinds of sources and not others?
- Which kinds of evidence are acceptable and why?

- What tools do I use to analyse and evaluate arguments and evidence?
- What constitutes an acceptable answer?

Now you are researching an academic topic of your own choice, it is the methodology rather than the theme which determines the scope of your research – the directions you go in and the limits to which you can find and analyse sources. It is still the case that you will locate and evaluate more than one perspective, and that the perspectives will differ in their arguments, evidence base, and possibly also their context and assumptions, but the ways in which these differ, and the limits of those differences, will be decided by how you have answered those questions of methodology.

ACTIVITY 9.06

Before reading about some specific types of research methodology, consider what you already know about the methodology of your chosen report question. Think about, discuss and write down your ideas about the following:

- Which kinds of sources are likely to be appropriate for my question, and which are likely not to be?
- What counts as acceptable evidence for my report?
- Which methods or techniques should I be using to analyse and evaluate sources?
- Based on my research so far, what kinds of conclusion are likely to be appropriate and which are not?

Another word for acceptability or appropriateness in this context is **validity**. A valid answer is one which is an answer which could reasonably be anticipated by the question which has been asked. As well as the sources you choose, it is the questions you ask about them which should determine the answers you can produce.

Reflection: When you have considered all of this, you can compare your answers with those of other students researching for their report, and also with the following three sections, which set out some starting points for research methodologies in the social sciences, sciences and arts and humanities.

Research methodologies in the social sciences

The social sciences form a diverse group of disciplines which are linked by their study of human behaviour and relationships. They include subjects such as sociology, psychology, economics, law, geography and anthropology. You may have studied some of these at school, although others are usually only studied as courses at university.

Research methodology in the social sciences is usually characterised as being systematic and **empirical**. This means that it will go through a logical series of steps in order to get the most accurate possible picture of human behaviour in any given situation. Research in the social sciences always aims to discover actions and behaviours which actually occur in the world, rather than turning inwards to the thoughts or feelings of the researcher.

The main division within the social sciences is between **quantitative** and **qualitative** approaches. Quantitative approaches assume that the data we can acquire about human beings is numerically measurable, and will focus on collecting data which can be analysed and evaluated in this way. This does not just mean directly collecting numerical data about size, weight or distance, it also means converting other kinds of response into numbers, such as by using a level of response scale to turn opinions and attitudes into numbers (for example, having a 5-point response scale, where strong agreement is recorded as 5 and strong disagreement as 1). Qualitative approaches, on the other hand, use interviews or other kinds of non-numerical observations to capture more detailed contextual information about attitudes and behaviour. Data collected in this way has a tendency to be more unique to a particular situation and less generalisable.

Other considerations in the social sciences involve the idea of **sampling**, where it is not possible to collect data on everyone who is experiencing something, so a subset of individuals are measured and calculations made to discover how reliably this can be extended to everyone in the same context. Because of this, much research in the social sciences is concerned with identifying studies that have been done of particular empirical situations, and then evaluating them to determine how reliable their data is, what it can be used for, and how reliably it can be used to draw further conclusions.

If your report is concerned with a debate which falls within the social sciences, the teacher supervising it is the best person to discuss appropriate methodologies. However, more detailed textbooks also exist which may provide useful additional information. It is worth bearing in mind, however, that these tend to be designed for university students, so may present too much detail and complexity for your report. Here are two examples:

Keith F. Punch, *Introduction to Social Research* (Sage, 2013)

Matthew David and Carole Sutton, *Social Research: An Introduction* (Sage, 2011)

Research methodologies in the natural sciences

Research in the natural sciences bears some similarities to research in the social sciences in that it is systematic and empirical. It is also, however, committed to **positivism**, which means that it assumes it can collect data which gives a true, numerically precise and reliable measurement of what is there. This means that qualitative data is not regarded as being valid.

KEY TERM

sampling: collecting a subset of data and then drawing conclusions about the items not collected, depending on the population

KEY TERM

positivism: the belief that anything must be positively observed and scientifically verified to be acceptable

As the phrase 'natural sciences' suggests, the object of study is the natural world, rather than human relationships and behaviours. Human beings are only studied as biological organisms which can be studied in the same way as other biological, physiological or biochemical systems in disciplines like biology, physiology or medicine. Research in the natural sciences also makes a distinction between **experimental** and **theoretical** findings. Experimental data is essential, as scientists are committed to the idea that we cannot know things about nature unless we measure them as exactly as possible, and have verifiable records of those measurements. Repeated experiments may then produce consistent findings about a particular type of **phenomenon**. In that case, it may then be possible to generalise that finding and predict what will occur when it is measured in the future, or in other contexts. We call this kind of prediction a **hypothesis**. Successfully proven hypotheses may then lead to theoretical knowledge: ideas about how something works which help us to predict the behaviour of phenomena which have not yet been observed but share similar or identical qualities. Once scientists are satisfied that this can be reliably done, it may lead to the formulation of a scientific law: a statement of a generally accepted aspect of the behaviour of the natural world. **Scientific models** are often used to help work out the precise parameters of a scientific law, as these are sets of predictions that help to explain and analyse a natural phenomenon which is still being fully investigated. Laws are also often validated by a mathematical analysis, as it is generally accepted by modern science that the Universe is constructed according to principles and relationships that are mathematical in nature: they are defined by numerical relationships.

Because of this, much of your research in the natural sciences will consist of identifying experimental observations which have been made of a specific phenomenon, and evaluating the methods used in order to draw conclusions about how trustworthy that data is, and the extent to which it can be used to draw further conclusions.

What is stated above can be applied in general to all research in the natural sciences, although your own research project may be more specifically concerned with physics, chemistry or biology. Which of these most applies will depend on the type of phenomenon you are investigating and how it is measured: whether it has to do with the nature of mass or energy, the composition of matter, or the study of living organisms. Some research may make links between these branches of science, such as biochemistry, the study of how the matter of which organisms are made produces the mechanisms of life, or how the nature of energy (physics) influences the composition of particular kinds of matter (chemistry). Many scientists increasingly make these links, or also point to the role of mathematics in describing all natural phenomena.

It is also important in this section to remind ourselves of what was said in Section 9.02 on identifying suitable debates. Given what we have set out here, a valid scientific research project would be to make a number of observations of a natural phenomenon using a verifiable method which would allow for the testing or construction of a model to explain that phenomenon, or that might corroborate other observations in order to make further progress towards the formulation of a scientific law. Here, more than one perspective would not exist, and although a good scientific project, it would not be a debate and would be unsuitable for the report.

If you are interested in doing a report within the natural sciences, it would be better to identify a situation where two competing models, or methods of measurement, exist, with recognised strengths and weaknesses in explaining a specific natural phenomenon but – as yet – no final consensus on which is the best one to use. Here you would then be able to analyse and evaluate the observations and other studies which support each model or method and treat them in this way as opposing perspectives.

experimental: data which comes from controlled observations of individual phenomena

theoretical: general ideas or rules which explain individual phenomena and are based on experimental data

phenomenon: something which occurs in the natural world

hypothesis: an assumption made to be tested against further investigation

scientific model: an idea used to represent something that happens in nature

Deconstruction

Reconstruction

Reflection

Communication

Again, your teacher will be able to advise you further on suitable methodologies in the sciences for your own research topic. The following textbook may also be helpful, although it is aimed at university students:

Michael P. Marder, *Research Methods for Science* (Cambridge University Press, 2011)

Research methodologies in the arts and humanities

Research methodologies in the arts and humanities tend to be very diverse, with a much lower level of agreement about what makes up a suitable methodology than there is in the social or natural sciences. Subjects which count within the arts and humanities include English literature, modern languages and literature, art and art history, Classics, cultural studies, media studies, philosophy and history, although some people working in some of these subjects may prefer to place them within the social sciences and use research methodologies based on qualitative (and sometimes even quantitative) data.

KEY TERM

Subjectivity: the view that meaning is based on individual beliefs and attitudes

Research in the arts and humanities which is not part of the social sciences tends to have in common a commitment to **subjectivity** in interpretation. This means that meaning is considered to be dependent on an individual's beliefs, attitudes or situation. This means that meaning is not fixed and can change over time. Another consequence is that it is perfectly possible that more than one interpretation is possible, and something can have several different, even conflicting, meanings simultaneously. Arguments in the arts and humanities are often focused on exploring different possible meanings without being committed to discovering one correct answer. Nuance and ambiguity are valued as opposed to definite answers.

If you are researching in this area, your work is likely to be focused on reading and interpreting meanings in written texts. One important distinction will be between primary and secondary texts. We first encountered this distinction in Section 2.05, as these make up different kinds of evidence. In the arts and humanities, primary texts may be things such as novels, poems, speeches, paintings or official documents from a specific historical period. These often have a number of different interpretations, and disagreements about what those interpretations could be. Secondary texts tend to be academic books or essays which contain arguments about those different interpretations, written by literary critics or historians. When you write your report you are effectively producing another secondary text with another set of interpretations or judgements to add to the debate. The arts and humanities are squarely focused on debates, so exploring different perspectives is usually not a problem for the report.

Depending on your exact subject area, you will need to discuss with your supervisor what the most appropriate tools for interpretation are, depending on the type of text with which you are dealing. For example, if you are working within English literature you may be using the techniques of close reading of imagery or prosodic analysis to explore meanings in a collection of poems. in history you may be analysing a piece of primary documentary evidence to make judgements about what it tells us about a historical event. In cultural or media studies you may use toolkits such as semiotics or discourse analysis to interpret visual or audiovisual texts more generally, or particular cultural practices. The important thing here is to decide why you are using a particular tool and what meanings it will allow you to uncover, or not. Often there is a debate within a particular subject over which interpretative tools have more value: in English literature, for example, there are disagreements over whether we should focus on closely reading the language of literature or place literary texts within their broader historical and cultural contexts. Knowing where your project locates itself within a question like this can be an important methodological insight upon which you can reflect. One good approach is to ensure you

Deconstruction

Reconstruction

Reflection

Communication

research secondary as well as primary texts – it is the secondary texts, and the arguments they make, which will allow you to locate a suitable debate, and test out the different conclusions against your own analysis of the primary texts. Writing about this process in your research log will help you to show a good understanding of methodology.

Discussion point

Talk with other students who are studying or researching in the same area as you. Describe in your own words what is different or significant about methodologies in that subject and what aspects are most applicable to the report.

9.05 Writing and referencing your report

Writing

When you come to write the report itself, it is helpful to think in terms of the different functions each part of the report needs to perform, whatever research methodology you have selected. These are:

- introducing your argument
- evaluating sources, arguments and evidence
- concluding your argument and reaching a final judgement.

These functions are similar to those of the essay in Component 2, and the report as a piece of writing builds on these skills. Because of this, it would be helpful to re-read Chapter 5 as you begin to type up your report. The 'Research Report Proposal Poster' below shows a poster which has been developed from the example headings for the question 'Is globalisation economically good for developed countries' after Activity 9.03.

Referencing

As you did for your essay for Component 2, you will need to produce a fully referenced final version of your report. This works in the same way for exactly the same reasons, so when you come to cite references in your report and write the bibliography, the guidance given on this in Section 5.05 is a good starting point.

The report differs in two ways, however, from other essay writing projects. Firstly, its scale is larger, with more sources to cite and reference. Secondly, it places more demands on the writer of the report to ensure that the system of referencing selected fits the content of the report.

The author-title system (footnotes)

In Chapter 5, we outlined the purposes of citation and referencing, alongside a summary of the Harvard system as one which could be used for the Component 2 essay as it was straightforward to implement and conveniently linked in-text citations to the bibliography at the end. It is not, however, the only system of referencing available to you. Another major alternative is the author-title system. This cites sources in the text using footnotes. These citations are then repeated as references in a bibliography at the end. Because it allows fuller information about the date, title and authorship of a source in the text of an essay (rather than just in the bibliography), the author-title system tends to be used more frequently in subjects like English literature, foreign literatures, history and philosophy. The author-date system (Harvard referencing) is more popular in the social sciences and sciences where the date of publication of a source (how current it is) is more important and needs to be more prominent. Because it focuses on author's name and date only, citations are relatively brief and can be placed within the text itself without being excessively distracting.

With the author-title system of footnoting, if you wish to cite a source you have paraphrased or quoted verbatim (using quotation marks) you should insert a footnote immediately after the source has been used. This is usually at the end of the sentence containing the quotation or paraphrase, following the full stop. If you have quoted more than a sentence of a source and indented it as a block quotation, then the footnote should immediately follow the end of the quotation. It is a good idea to learn the menu operation or keyboard shortcut on your word-processing software which allows you to insert a footnote in order to do this easily.

Books

Books should be cited in footnotes in the following way. If you are referring to a specific page (as you probably will be in these disciplines), then that should follow the citation:

Jeffrey Sachs, *The End of Poverty* (London: Penguin, 2005), 55.

It is also possible to add important information about the differences between the original date of publication and that of a modern edition, and the modern edition's editor.

Tennessee Williams, *A Streetcar Named Desire*, eds. Patricia Hern and Michael Hooper (1947; London: Bloomsbury, 1984), 109.

Generally, the order is author, title, then in brackets place of publication, publisher and date of publication, then the page reference.

Subsequent footnote citations of the same source can take a shortened form:

Sachs, *The End of Poverty*, 82.

If you are referring to a specific point made in a source, or quoting from it, and your source has page numbers, then you must always give it.

Articles in academic journals, newspapers and magazines

Generally speaking, these have the following structure: Author, Article Title, Periodical Title, volume/issue (year), page extent. For example:

David Dawson, 'Against the Divine Ventroliquist: Coleridge and de Man on Symbol, Allegory, and Scripture', *Literature and Theology: An International Journal of Theory, Criticism and Culture* 4 (1990), 293–310.

Subsequent footnotes for this article would be as follows:

Dawson, 'Against the Divine Ventroliquist', 300.

Electronic Sources

Most of the sources you are likely to encounter will be electronic, whether they are newspaper, journal or magazine articles, or electronic copies of books. Using the author-title system, you can cite from them in footnotes using the following general form:

Author or editor name, 'Title of article or section used', *Title of overall work*, (date created, published or placed online [day month year]). Medium. <web URL>, page range or online equivalent. (Date accessed).

For an article published in a periodical online, this is how the general form would look as a specific example:

D. Shariatmadari, 'The death of a language', *The Guardian*, (5 February 2010). Online. Available from: http://www.guardian.co.uk/commentisfree/2010/feb/05/bo-language-extinct-linguistics. (Accessed 16 January 2016).

If no author is given, then the reference should be organised with the title first.

'Legal wrangle puts India's generic drugs at risk', *New Scientist*, (29 January 2013). Online. Available from: http://www.newscientist.com/article/dn11053-legal-wrangle-puts-indias-generic-drugs-at-risk.html. (Accessed 16 January 2016).

The bibliography

Even if you use a system based on footnoting you will still need a bibliography at the end. This lists all of your sources in alphabetical order, with the surname first, followed by a comma and their first name or initials. The rest of the entry is as for the footnotes (without including specific page references). References to more than one text by the same author should use a long dash instead of repeating the author's name:

Dawson, David. 'Against the Divine Ventriloquist: Coleridge and de Man on Symbol, Allegory, and Scripture', *Literature and Theology: An International Journal of Theory, Criticism and Culture* 4 (1990), 293–310.

'Legal wrangle puts India's generic drugs at risk', *New Scientist*, 29 January 2013. Online. Available from: http://www.newscientist.com/article/dn11053-legal-wrangle-puts-indias-generic-drugs-at-risk.html. (Accessed 16 January 2016).

Sachs, Jeffrey. *The End of Poverty* (London: Penguin, 2005).

Williams, Tennessee. *A Streetcar Named Desire*, eds. Patricia Hern and Michael Hooper (1947; London: Bloomsbury, 1984).

Shariatmadari, D. 'The death of a language', *The Guardian*, (5 February 2010). Online. Available from: http://www.guardian.co.uk/commentisfree/2010/feb/05/bo-language-extinct-linguistics. (Accessed 16 January 2016).

The bibliography should be indicated by the subheading 'Bibliography', centred on the page.

Other systems of citation and referencing

Harvard in-text and the author-title footnoting systems are not the only options you have. A number of others also exist, and are associated with particular subject areas:

- Vancouver system (a variant of author-title footnotes)
- MLA (often used in literary studies, with in-text and footnote variants)

- Chicago style (used across a range of subject areas, and also with in-text and footnote variants)
- APA style (an in-text system similar to Harvard which is frequently used in science research)

Part of your task when doing research for your report is to think about the referencing needs of your project and which system might be most suitable. You should record your thinking and decision-making in your research log and also involve your teacher in this too. When you have decided on a style it is very important that you find a reliable guide to applying it and do so accurately and consistently. A well-kept research log and set of notes on sources will be crucial here as this will keep a record of information about sources so you have everything you need to cite and reference them.

ACTIVITY 9.07

Consider the subject area of your report and the kind of information you need to record about your sources. This might include the following questions:

- Is there an established system of referencing linked to that subject?
- Is the date of each source, its title or other information about it the most important aspect of the source for me?
- Am I likely to wish to use footnotes to record additional information about some of the sources I cite?

Based on this, decide which referencing system you might want to use and why for your report, and discuss your proposed choice with your teacher.

9.06 What happens next?

Chapter 1 began by defining the difference between skills and knowledge, and exploring the ways in which Global Perspectives & Research and the Critical Path have been constructed to test and develop your skills for learning. The Partnership for 21st Century Learning (www.p21. org) has set out a 'framework for learning' of the skills and knowledge needed to succeed in work and in life in the 21st century which lines up with much of what this course is designed to support. It is made up of the following elements:

- **content knowledge**: English, languages, arts, mathematics, economics, science, geography, history, economics and more
- **learning and innovation skills**: creativity and innovation, thinking critically and solving problems, communication, collaboration
- **information, media and technology skills**: information literacy, media literacy, ICT literacy
- **life and career skills**: flexibility and adaptability, initiative and self-direction, social and cross-cultural skills, productivity and accountability, leadership and responsibility.

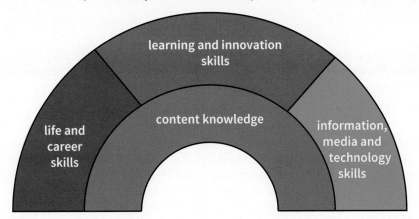

When following the Critical Path through the first three components (the written paper, essay and team project), you were progressively building elements of learning and innovation skills, supported by information, media and technology skills as you carried out research to locate information and used media and ICT to support your writing and presentations. Life and career skills were also an increasing part of this, as you worked by yourself on each individual outcome as well as with others to show leadership while being responsible and accountable to a team.

The report develops these skills in even more detail, as you are still following the Critical Path in order to locate and read sources, and put them together into a written argument. This relies on your learning and innovation skills: to think critically, solve problems and to communicate. Some of the life and career skills will have been particularly developed, however, as you need to show much more initiative and self-direction to manage yourself through the process of identifying, researching and writing your own individual project over a number of months, with much less direct intervention by your teacher. This will also test your productivity (your ability to efficiently produce a planned outcome) and your accountability (your responsibility for what you have committed to deliver).

Deconstruction

Reconstruction

Reflection

Communication

In addition to this, the report bridges the gap between the three sets of 21st-century skills and the areas of content knowledge which are also vital for a student in this century. By selecting a specific academic subject for your report, you will be learning to make the links between content you have learnt and your developing abilities to think critically about it, solve problems which emerge and be creative and innovative in seeking out new knowledge. In order to do this, you will be relying even more on your flexibility, your ability to direct yourself and your sense of personal responsibility for your own outcomes. This combination of skills and knowledge will not just help you to make a success of your report, it is also the package of qualities which universities look for in their students, and employers when they are recruiting. In this way, Global Perspectives & Research will not only have supported you well with your studies at this stage, it will have prepared you effectively for the next step in your life, whatever that may be.

Summary

In this chapter we have:

- outlined the formal expectations and requirements of the research report, and how they relate to what you need to produce and how it will be assessed

- reflected on the skills you have developed doing Global Perspectives & Research so far, and assessed how you will re-use and develop these for the research report

- learnt how to apply your skills of reflection to reflect on the process of your research

- examined an example of a research log and considered how one should be used to support your report

- discussed the difference between the use of themes and methodologies in the Component 2 essay and the report in defining opposing perspectives

- explained how research methodologies operate differently in the social sciences, sciences and arts and humanities, and the implications of this for your report and how you write it

- outlined how to effectively structure your writing in your report

- explored how to use citation and referencing appropriately depending on the subject area of your report

- compared the skills you have learnt on this course to 21st-century skills for students

- discussed how you could apply your learning from producing the research report to your other courses, and to what you do next, including at university.

When you have completed this chapter, you should feel confident about the process of choosing, researching and writing your report. You should also be able to clearly see the process you have gone through in the Global Perspectives & Research course as a whole, and how the different tasks and skills relate to the whole Critical Path. That path comes together most strongly in your work for the report, and it should also help you to see beyond the Global Perspectives & Research course, using what you have learnt to make links with the other subjects you are doing and enhancing your independent, critical learning skills ready for university and the workplace.

Glossary

Ability to observe: how far a source has first-hand knowledge of the things it argues about

Academic: related to something studied at school or college, or related to studying and thinking, not practical activity or personal interests

Agenda: a list of the items to be covered in a meeting which is produced in advance. It also usually includes the time and location of the meeting and who will be attending.

Ambiguity: the existence of several different specific meanings for a single term, all of which may be equally possible

Analogy: the use of one thing to explain or define something else

Analysis: breaking down something you are studying into smaller parts in order to understand it more clearly

Argument: one or more reasons leading to a conclusion

Argument indicator: a term used specifically to signpost the reasons or conclusions in an argument

Assertion: an unsupported claim

Assumption: an unstated reason which needs to be included in order for an argument to work successfully

Audience: the group of people at which a performance or piece of writing is aimed

Bias: a view of something which deliberately favours one particular aspect or opinion

Bibliography: a list at the end of the essay of works that have been cited

Broadsheet: newspaper traditionally printed on a larger sheet of newsprint, but now found both in print and online. It usually contains articles of serious general interest.

Citation: identifying where you have used material from someone else in your own writing

Claim: a statement which may or may not be true

Clarification by contrast: clarifying the meaning of a term by contrasting it with what it is not in order to narrow down the possible range of things it could be understood as

Clarification by example: clarifying a term by giving examples of what it is, or what it is not, in order to help the reader understand what is being described

Command word: in an imperative, the words which contain the command or commands to which the reader should respond. Examples might include 'show' or 'evaluate'.

Conclusion: a claim about the world which we are asked to accept based on reasons

Content word: words in an essay which show the key content which is being focused on in each paragraph

Context: factors that are outside the source and its argument, such as its author or where it was published, that affect its meaning

Contextualisation: establishing the background and significance of a question before embarking on an argument

Counter-argument: an argument which could be made to challenge another argument

Creativity: an original, unusual, new or imaginative approach to presenting your arguments

Credibility: the believability of the claims made by a source related to its context

Debate: the confrontation of opposing views on an issue, where each tries to show they are more convincing than the others

Declarative: a question which is phrased as a statement, outlining a situation to be described or explored

Decoding: reading texts by mapping the marks on the page to specific meanings. Revealing the meaning is like breaking a code.

Dictionary definition: the definition of a term found in a dictionary, describing its usage in ordinary language

Effective: a solution which has a measurable impact in changing a situation you have researched in a real-world situation

Empathy: acquiring a fuller understanding of a perspective other than one's own by giving it sufficient space to be considered

Empirical: research that is focused on measuring data about the external world

Essay conclusion: final section of an essay, which reaches and supports a final judgement

Essay introduction: opening paragraph of an essay, which clarifies key terms in the question, contextualises the issues involved and sets up a line of argument

Essay model: a suggested pattern for a piece of writing, and which you can use to evaluate your own writing

Evaluation: identifying the strengths and weaknesses of something in order to make a judgement about it

Evidence: facts or other data supporting reasons or claims

Experimental: data which comes from controlled observations of individual phenomena

Expert definition: a definition from an expert in the field which represents a meaning for the term based on specialist knowledge

Expertise: the specific knowledge or learning a source has about the area in which it is arguing

Facts: measurements of things which are accepted to actually exist, and which can be proved or disproved

Gaze: the ways in which eye contact is directed towards others in order to communicate

Gesture: the use of hand and arm positions and movements to communicate meaning

Global: the world as a whole, either looked at overall, or compared in its diversity

Hypothesis: an assumption made to be tested against further investigation

Imperative: a question which is phrased as a command, asking the reader to do something specific

Inferential gap: the gap of reasoning between a reason and the conclusion it supports

Innovative: a solution which you can show is different to other solutions which have been used to deal with a problem

Intermediate conclusion: a conclusion which also functions as a reason leading to the main conclusion. It is supported by reasons within a specific section of an argument.

Interrogative: a question framed directly as a question, requiring an answer where a number of alternative answers usually exist. The answer given is usually phrased as a conclusion, supported by reasons and evidence.

Issue: a specific, more narrowly defined, area within a topic which is more suitable for an essay or other piece of work

Key word: individual word or phrase which can be focused upon in order to refine or clarify understanding of a particular topic or area

Knowledge: our understanding of facts or other information

Line of argument: a separate direction or type of argument which leads to the conclusion

Local: specific places in the world looked at individually. These might be villages, towns, regions or countries.

Main body: the section of the essay between the introduction and conclusion, introducing, developing and contrasting perspectives

Main conclusion: the final conclusion of an argument

Methodology: the study of the most appropriate methods to use to research and develop knowledge in a specific subject area

Minutes: a written record of what was discussed in a meeting under each of the agenda points and any agreed points for action after the meeting, with who is to do each and by when. One of the people attending the meeting is usually given the task of producing the minutes.

Neutrality: the degree to which a source either shows balance or deliberately selects argument and evidence in order to support a particular case

Non-verbal communication: communication using the body which does not involve words

Opinions: an individual's judgement of the value of something. These cannot be proved or disproved, but can be challenged by other opinions

Paralanguage: deliberate non-verbal variation of sound from the vocal tract to support and modify verbal communication

Paraphrase: using material from a source in your own words

Perspective: a coherent world view which responds to an issue, made up of argument, evidence, assumptions, and perhaps also from a particular context

Phenomenon: something which occurs in the natural world

Position: how a body is positioned in a space, especially in relation to other people

Positivism: the belief that anything must be positively observed and scientifically verified to be acceptable

Practice: the specific experience of doing something

Primary evidence: first-hand information, directly about something

Purpose: the intended outcome of a performance or piece of writing

Qualitative: data that is based on attitudes and opinions and cannot be reduced to numbers

Qualitative evidence: evidence which measures the quality of something as attributes which cannot be summarised as numerical quantities

Quantitative: data that is numerically measurable

Quantitative evidence: evidence which measures the amount of something, usually numerically

Question stem: a word starting a question, such as *what, how, is, should* or *can,* which controls the type of question which is asked and the range of possible responses

Reason: a claim used to support a conclusion

Referencing: giving details of how to locate sources you have cited

Reflection: consciously considering what we have read or experienced and being able to explain the effect it has had on the way we think, feel or act; evaluating an action which has already been completed in order to understand it more fully and to undertake it more effectively in the future

Reliability: the extent to which a piece of evidence provides acceptable support for a claim or reason

Reputation: the past actions or arguments made by a source which have an influence on their current credibility

Research: searching out information on a topic

Research proposal: a short written summary of the intended content of your research report, with the areas your research will cover

Rhetoric: language which is primarily designed to persuade its reader or listener, rather than using rational techniques of argument to demonstrate the strength of the case it wishes to make

Sampling: collecting a subset of data and then drawing conclusions about the items not collected, depending on the population

Scanning: very quickly searching through a large volume of information for specific key words or phrases

Scientific model: an idea used to represent something that happens in nature

Secondary evidence: evidence combined or summarised from primary evidence, but not directly from the situation itself

Signpost: word or phrase in an essay which shows the reader the direction in which the argument is going

Skills: any mental or physical abilities you can improve through practising them

Skimming: quickly moving through an individual source in order to pick out clues to its content and purpose

Stipulated definition: a definition that is declared, or stipulated, as the one that should be used for the context being described

Strength: a feature of an argument which makes it more likely it will be accepted

Structure: the organisation of a text, and how each element within it is placed together

Subjectivity: the view that meaning is based on individual beliefs and attitudes

Synthesis: combining more than one thing together in order to understand them more effectively by exploring their differences and similarities

Tabloid: newspaper traditionally printed on a smaller sheet of newsprint, but now found both in print and online. It contains articles which are sensationalist or part of the popular media.

Theme: approach to a topic, particularly the seven listed in the Cambridge International AS & A Level Global Perspectives & Research syllabus. The combination of a theme with a topic can help to define a perspective on that topic.

Theoretical: general ideas or rules which explain individual phenomena and are based on experimental data

Theory: a general set of ideas which is used to explain why we experience things in specific ways

Therefore test: a technique which inserts the word *therefore* into a text to test whether or not it is an argument

Thesis-antithesis-synthesis: approach to essay writing which involves establishing a perspective, exploring one that opposes it, then reaching a synthesis, or combination, between the two

Topic: an area for study, as defined in the list of topics in the Cambridge International AS & A Level Global Perspectives & Research

Topic sentence: the first sentence of a paragraph which summarises its content, including the argument it presents

Vagueness: a term is vague when it has a range of meaning which cannot be reduced to one or more specific meanings.

Validity: an acceptable or reasonable answer to the question that has been asked

Verbatim citation: using the exact words from a source, indicated by quotation marks

Vested interest: the direct benefit a source would gain from having its conclusions accepted by others

Weakness: a feature of an argument which makes it less likely it will be accepted

Index